Teaching Singing to Children
and Young Adults

Teaching Singing to Children and Young Adults

Jenevora Williams

compton
PUBLISHING

Compton Publishing

This edition first published 2013 © 2013 by Compton Publishing Ltd.

Registered office: Compton Publishing Ltd, 30 St. Giles', Oxford, OX1 3LE, UK
Registered company number: 07831037

Editorial offices: 49 Bath Street, Abingdon, Oxfordshire OX14 1EA, UK

Web: www.comptonpublishing.co.uk

ISBN 978-1-909082-00-7

A catalogue record for this book is available from the British Library.

Cover image: Harry Venning, http://www.harryvenning.co.uk/
Cover design: David Siddall, http://www.davidsiddall.com
Graphic designs: Milton Mermikides, http://www.miltonline.com
Set in 11pt Weiss by Regent Typesetting, London

1   2013

'Careful the things you say,
Children will listen.
Careful the things you do,
Children will see
And learn.
Children may not obey,
But children will listen.
Children will look to you
For which way to turn,
To learn what to be.
Careful before you say,
'Listen to me'.
Children will listen.'

Stephen Sondheim

Contents

Foreword xv

Using this book xvi

About the author xviii

Acknowledgements xix

Prelude: questioning the assumptions xx

    The role of the singing teacher xxiv

Chapter 1: Why sing and why teach singing to children? 1

1.1   What is singing? 1

     Communication 2

     Musicianship 3

     Technique 3

     Repertoire 4

1.2   Singing is good for your mental and physical health 4

1.3   Why do children need to learn vocal technique? 7

     How do children train to become high achievers in physical

     activities? 12

1.4   Differences between girls and boys 13

Chapter 1 Summary 15

Interlude A: Singing in tune 16

Chapter 2: Children from birth to 6 years 20

2.1 The musical experience of the unborn baby 20

2.2 Early singing, carer and infant 22

2.3 Musical and language development 22

2.4 Musical play 23

2.5 Educational development 24

2.6 Physical development 25
  The vocal structure of the infant 25
  The vocal structure of the young child 28

2.7 Singing technique: what can and can't be done 30
  Posture 30
  Breathing 30
  Pitch range and voice timbre 31
  Singing in tune 32

2.8 The relationship between parents and teachers 33

Chapter 2 Summary 34

Interlude B: The learning process 35

Chapter 3: Children aged 7 to 12 years 44

3.1 Context 44

3.2 Physical development 45

3.3 Musical development 46
  Reading musical notation 46

3.4 Singing in tune 47

3.5 Singing technique: what can and can't be done 49
  Repertoire 50

3.6 The relationship between parents and teachers 51

Chapter 3 Summary 52

Interlude C: The child as a professional singer 53

Chapter 4: Adolescents 55

4.1   Context 55

4.2   Singing technique: why teach it? 57

4.3   Onset of puberty 57

4.4   Adolescent girls 59
Physical development of the voice 59
Technique: what the girl's voice can and can't do 60

4.5   Adolescent boys 61
Physical development of the voice 61
   Possible signs of change to Cooksey Stages I and II 63
Technique: what the boy's voice can and can't do 64
   Assess the voice 64
   Should a boy continue to sing with his high pitch-range? 65
   Puberphonia 67
Repertoire for teenage boys 68
Historical background to singing during adolescent voice change ... 69
Counter-tenors or male altos 72

4.6   Allocation of choral parts to voices that are changing 72
Girls: soprano or alto? 73
Boys: tenor or bass? 74

4.7   The role of parents in singing lessons for adolescents 74

Chapter 4 Summary 76

Interlude D: Operatic repertoire for ages 18 to 21 78

Chapter 5: How the voice works 80

5.1   Introduction 80

5.2   Posture and breathing 81
What is 'support'? 86
What is the role of the diaphragm? 87

5.3   The primary sound source: the larynx 88
The vocal folds 90
Chest and head registers 92

Falsetto...92

Vibrato 93

Creak 94

Constriction...94

Onset 96

Breathiness..97

Pitch range 99

Register change..99

Belting...100

5.4 The vocal tract: the throat, mouth and nose 101

Swallowing 103

Yawning...103

The shape of the pharynx in singing 103

Jaw tension..104

The tongue 106

Projected resonance...107

Nasality 108

Vowels..109

Vowel problems 111

Consonants 112

Consonant problems 113

The lips and facial expression 113

5.5 From Mozart to musical theatre, gospel to pop:
     cross-training for the voice 114

Chapter 5 Summary 117

Interlude E: Vocal tract acoustics – resonance and
formants...119

Chapter 6: Structuring lessons and practice 123

6.1 Individual lesson structure 123

Physical and emotional empathy 125

Notebooks and recordings 127

6.2 Physical skills: athletes' training principles.................127

Training must be specific 128

Overload the system...128

Train progressively...129
Balance hard and easy training...129
Vary the training...129
Train regularly...129
Rest 129

6.3 Warm-ups: why are they necessary and how do we do them? .. 130
Introduction...130
The theory behind warming-up 131
The framework for a warm-up 133
    Wake up and balance the body..133
    Breathing..134
    Release the throat 135
    Warm-up the larynx 136
    Explore resonance 136
    Clarify articulation 137

6.4 Private practice...138
Motivation to practise 138
Personal practice routine 139
    Set up your mind 139
    Align your body...139
    Remember to breathe 140
    Warm up your larynx 141
    Technical exercises..141
    Familiar repertoire 141
    New repertoire 141
    Know when to stop..141
    Warm-down 141

6.5 Memorisation of music...142
Techniques for improving your memorisation skills.......................143

Chapter 6 Summary 145

Interlude F: Child protection issues............................... 147

Chapter 7: Vocal health and ill health 149

7.1 Why good voice use is important 149
Voice problems in children..149
Prevention of voice problems...150
The need to raise vocal volume 151
Not enough variety in voice use................................152
Voice use while under emotional stress 152
Speaking or vocalising during physical exercise.......153
Exposure to irritants 153
Poor acoustic conditions..153
Pacing the voice...154

7.2 Lifestyle issues affecting vocal health for all singers: teachers and
pupils 155
Eating and drinking...155
Medications 158

7.3 What to do when the voice goes wrong 159
Voice first aid 159

7.4 Voice disorders in children 160
Organic voice disorders (not related to voice use)...........160
Functional voice disorders (related to voice use) 160
Contextual or environmental factors...............................161
Why intensive training sometimes goes wrong...............162
Professional adult musicians 163
Children who are trained to sing at a professional level..............164

7.5 Performance expectations, anxieties and catastrophe theory.... 166
Strategies for anxiety management..................................168

7.6 Golden rules for healthy voice use 169

Chapter 7 Summary 170

Interlude G: Choral singing 173

Chapter 8: Children with specific individual needs.............. 178

Some general guidance for the teacher 181
Baseline assessment 181
Encouragement and confidence..................................181
Multi-sensory learning 181
Short-term memory 182
Long-term memory 182
Avoiding distractions...182
Clear practice structure 183
Reading music..183

8.1 Dyslexia, dyscalculia and dyspraxia 184

8.2 Autism and Asperger's syndrome 185
Some helpful approaches for the teacher with pupils on the
autistic spectrum...187

8.3 ADD or ADHD.. 188
Some helpful approaches for the teacher with a pupil with
ADHD..188

8.4 Asthmatics... 189
Guidelines for teachers of an asthmatic pupil 189

8.5 Eczema 189

8.6 Fatigue-related conditions 190

8.7 Hearing impairment... 190
Some helpful approaches for the teacher of children with
hearing impairment..191

8.8 Visual impairment 191
Specific eye conditions: tracking problems such as nystagmus 192
Albinism...192

8.9 Cerebral palsy 193

8.10 Down's syndrome 193

8.11 Cystic fibrosis... 194
Some helpful approaches for the teacher of the pupil with
cystic fibrosis 194

Chapter 8 Summary 195

Interlude H: Historical outline of singing training for children.. 196

Postlude 200

Glossary 202

Phonetic symbols 211

Recommended further reading by subject area 212

References.. 215

Index 219

Foreword

It is a great pleasure to have the opportunity to provide a foreword to Jenevora Williams' book *Teaching Singing to Children and Young Adults*. The text represents the culmination of years of successful practice, allied to recent systematic research, into key aspects of how singing develops from childhood through adolescence and into early adulthood. An accomplished singer and teacher, Jenevora builds on her extensive craft knowledge and doctoral-level research to provide an evidence-based account of how we can best foster singing development by ensuring that pedagogical practice is closely linked to the physical nature of the vocal instrument. This is an interdisciplinary approach that offers a teacher-friendly synthesis in an engaging and enlightened narrative with helpful (and often amusing) illustrations and case studies. It is always a challenge to capture the process of singing teaching in written form because of its moment-to-moment interweaving of action, response and interpretation. Jenevora is to be commended for providing us with a multi-level account of how we can ensure that successful singing is not the province of a privileged minority, but open to all if we adopt appropriate teaching strategies.

Professor Graham Welch
Established Chair of Music Education, Institute of Education, London
President, International Society of Music Education (ISME)
Chair, Society for Education, Music and Psychology Research (SEMPRE)

Using this book

The first chapter is an introduction to singing and music teaching; some common teaching advice is questioned in the light of research evidence. Chapters 2, 3 and 4 have information dealing with the abilities of young singers at different developmental stages. They outline the physical growth patterns as well as the developmental phases; this information is useful for the teacher in order to know the limitations as well as the possibilities of pupils at different ages. Chapter 5 is the core of the book; you will find there an outline of the workings of the voice. As the function of each part of the vocal system is described, this is then applied directly to singing technique. Each aspect of singing technique has vocal exercises to go with it. After this, the chapters deal with specific issues: these are vocal health, lesson or practice structure and some strategies to enable singing lessons to include children with different physical or educational needs. Between each chapter is an interlude. These can be viewed as separate articles: related to the preceding chapter content, but also able to be read independently.

For the purposes of easy definition within this book I refer to infants, children, adolescents and young adults.

- The **infant** is under 1 year of age.
- A **child** is from the age of 1 year to the onset of puberty.
- An **adolescent** is from the onset of puberty to the age of about 18.
- A **young adult** is from the age of about 18 to the mid-20s.

Until the mid-20s, the voice can be considered as noticeably developing and changing. Although there are continuous changes in the voice, these become steadier and slower during the adult singing life.

Pitches are defined by the letter name and the octave starting from C. For example, middle C is C4, one tone higher is D4, a semitone lower is B3, and C an octave higher is C5.

The International Phonetic Alphabet, or IPA, is a universal system for describing the sounds that make up our speech. Vowel sounds are defined by their phonetic symbol to avoid any confusion or ambiguity. For those readers who may be unfamiliar with the IPA, there is a key to the symbols used at the back of the book.

Most of the time, unless specified, the information given will apply to both girls and boys. The use of 'his' or 'her' is arbitrary and inter-changeable.

Throughout the text I have used case studies to illustrate various points. These all concern people I have taught or worked with; the stories are true but the names have been changed.

Young singers will generally want to sing in a variety of styles. It is an impossible task to define and group all musical styles and keep everyone happy. In this book the term Classical covers all Western art music from the Renaissance to the present day. The term Contemporary Commercial Music or CCM [1] covers pretty much everything else: musical theatre, pop, rock, gospel, folk and jazz.

This book is structured to enable the reader to move around, dipping in and out, according to specific interests or requirements. As a result of making the chapters able to stand more independently, there may be some repetition between them.

About the author

This book has arisen out of my personal fascination with people: how their voices work, how to get them to work at their optimum, why they sometimes don't work as well as they could, how they develop throughout the lifespan and how the personality of the singer is at the core of the whole process. I was a professional solo singer for many years, working in opera, oratorio and recitals. I had always taught alongside performing and gradually my interest in teaching overtook that of performing. After ten years of a busy touring performance schedule, I shifted the balance towards teaching and have found it endlessly fascinating and rewarding.

As a singing teacher, I work with people of all ages and abilities. I teach professional adult singers, pupils who are training to be professionals and amateur singers. I teach classical, musical theatre and pop. As well as dealing with healthy voices, I do specific rehabilitation work with singers from the hospital voice clinic: these individuals come under all of the categories mentioned above. I also teach children and have done so for over 20 years. I have been extremely fortunate to have taught in a variety of excellent institutions: music conservatoires, specialist music schools, theatre schools, cathedral choir schools, state schools and independent schools. Working with such a diverse group of pupils has been a real privilege and has given me many opportunities to think about the teaching process. In addition to practical teaching work I have been involved in voice research. This means working with laryngologists, acousticians, electrical engineers, anatomists, speech therapists, statisticians and educational theorists, all of them experts in their fields and all fascinated by voices.

Acknowledgements

I would like to finish this preamble with some acknowledgements. With each clever or innovative idea I have, I soon discover that I was not the first one to get there. This book is mainly based on information I have gleaned over the years from great teachers and researchers to whom I am eternally indebted. These include Graham Welch, David Howard, Janice Chapman, Johan Sundberg, Ingo Titze, Ron Morris, Gillyanne Kayes, Tom Harris, Christian Herbst, Felicity Cook, Stuart Barr, Heather Keens, Frith Trezevant, Veronica Campbell and my colleagues in the National Youth Choirs of Great Britain. Sally-Anne Zimmerman was a great help with the chapter on teaching children with special educational needs. Many friends and colleagues helped with proof-reading and general comments, especially John and Judith LeGrove. I particularly need to thank Noel McPherson for his encouragement and support in taking on this book and seeing it through to publication. I could not have written this book without the solitary retreats offered by Marguerite Farthing, Fiona Sampson and Marian Ash. On another practical level I have relied heavily on my mother, Caroline Williams and my neighbour Sara Scott, who have provided hours of childcare and numerous family meals. My husband, Stephen Goss is a ruthless critic and my strongest supporter. My biggest thanks are to him and to Lily and Jim.

Finally, I have been continually sustained by the inspiration gained from my singing pupils. Without this constant stimulation I would not have maintained the ongoing fascination that I have with the human voice.

Prelude: questioning the assumptions

'It is a mark of an educated mind to be able to entertain a thought without accepting it.' Aristotle

Humans are resourceful and curious. When presented with evidence we will make assumptions about cause and effect. If this evidence is limited, the assumptions may be flawed. Think of the Black Death travelling from China, through Europe and into Britain in the fourteenth century. Initially it was believed that this was due to the conjunction of three planets in 1345, causing 'great pestilence in the air'. Many years later, a link between the presence of rats and the disease was established, suggesting that rats were responsible. Later, further evidence linked the disease to the fleas that lived on the rats. Recent research has concluded that the bacterium *Yersinia pestis* was present in the fleas, which were carried by the rats. The recent researchers are no more intelligent than the astronomers of the fourteenth century; they merely have more evidence on which to base their conclusions.

The voice is inside the body; we can't see much of what is happening, so teachers have tended to base their methods on how it feels. Teaching anyone to sing has always been a subjective process: intelligent and curious teachers have devised methods and theories founded on their experience. This approach has, of course, produced fantastic singers, despite the limited evidence base. Perhaps a re-evaluation of singing pedagogy, with the advantage of more information, would help some of the singers who develop problems with their voices, or those who are just less able than others. Nowadays teachers can't use ignorance as an excuse; we can draw on a huge range of knowledge. With modern techniques of voice analysis and internal observation we can begin to understand more about how we sing. The science of x-rays, MRI scanning, spectral and waveform analysis, electroglottograms and laryngoscopy have contributed to our knowledge of vocal function. Scientific evidence can illuminate much of our accepted teaching practice, so that we are able to separate out the more useful and effective traditional voice training methods. Of course, this is all work in progress. Research and the pursuit of knowledge and understanding have not stopped yet, and never will do. There is still much that we don't know about voices and how they work. Our current understanding is merely based on the evidence we have here and now.

This book seeks to question every aspect of children's voices and methods of teaching singing that we may have assumed to be correct. If they can stand up to scrutiny in the light of the most recent evidence, then they are the best we can have for the moment.

There are many commonly held beliefs that may not withstand this reassessment. Here are some examples of widely accepted ideas that are being challenged.

1 *'Babies can cry for hours and their voices don't get tired – surely we could learn from them?'*
Babies have a completely different vocal set-up from children and adults. Their needs are specific to them and so the function of the voice isn't really comparable. Their prime concern for survival is to make noise to attract attention (short, loud, but not necessarily varied) and to feed efficiently (large quantities in little time); their vocal set-up fulfils this need excellently. Children and adults have developed the ability to form a huge variety of vocal sounds, enabling speech. Sustained speech (and singing) is helped by having larger lungs; these are needed for activities such as running. Infants have smaller lungs, and a larynx with different proportions, sitting higher in the throat. Young children have a vocal system that is part way between the infant and the adult model. Understanding this can help us to see why children's voices are not like mini-adult voices (p. 25).

2 *'Sing from your diaphragm'*
The diaphragm can neither be seen nor felt either internally or externally. Furthermore, it is working when we inhale, not when we make sound. This implies that any mention of the diaphragm is of little use for singing, the muscles we are consciously using for breathing are mostly abdominal ones (pp. 84–87).

3 *'Warming up should start with stretching exercises'*
Sports science suggests that it can be damaging to stretch cold muscles. For the singer, stretching includes singing sustained high notes as well

as overall body stretches. An effective warm-up needs to work the body gently in order to increase blood flow to the muscles; it also raises the muscle temperature, enabling better metabolic function. Overall body movements such as jogging or dancing are the best way to prepare muscles for action; this can be followed by gentle breathing and vocal exercises (pp. 131–133).

4 'Place the sound in the resonators at the front of the face (in the mask)'

The sound is made in the larynx and comes out through the mouth. It only goes into the nasal cavities if you sing with a nasal quality (usually reserved for nasal consonants, French nasal vowels or dramatic characterisation). The singer may feel a sensation of vibrations in the front of the face, if this happens when the voice is working well, then it can be a useful reminder to the singer. If the singer feels no particular sensation here it is simply because there are no special cavities in the skull for aiding vocal resonance (pp. 107–109).

5 'Children shouldn't be taught singing technique, it may damage their voices'

Learning a technique for any physical skill is merely discovering how to do the task with the least effort. If technique is taught at the right level for the individual, it will make singing easier and more enjoyable for her. It is rare for singing to cause pathological damage to the voice. The more common problem for singers is entrenched bad habits, which can remain throughout life. These bad habits can arise from either poor tuition, or just from a lack of guidance. For example, it's very unlikely that a singer will acquire good breathing technique without some help from a teacher. If the child is taught skills from a young age, they will be able to enjoy singing to the best of their ability (pp. 7–12).

6 'Singing is best done with an open throat, a yawning sensation may help'

The throat is a very versatile squeezy tube. The wrong constrictions will limit flexibility, add unnecessary tension and may result in a less-pleasant sound. The right constrictions allow us to form all of our vowels and consonants, as well as the exciting upper partials in the sound. The secret is, of course, to know the difference between them. A yawning action will lift the soft palate (good) and depress the back of the tongue (not good), pushing it down onto the top of the larynx. This reduces the mobility of the larynx and can result in a hooty sound. It can also limit the release of the jaw and rise of the soft palate. Any tongue tension will prevent clear articulation of vowels and consonants (pp. 106–107).

7 'Sing badly and you'll get nodules'

Vocal fold nodules rarely have a single cause, they tend to occur as a result of a combination of factors: the most common of which is anxiety, the most unlikely is bad singing technique. They can occur as a result of poor voice use in other contexts such as sport or unsupervised singing. Of all vocal fold pathologies, nodules are relatively easy to treat (p. 160).

8 'Boys and girls have different voices'

You may think that, in general, girls are better at singing. It has also been said that the sound of a high-quality boys' choir cannot be matched by that of a girls' choir. Research has shown that even experts couldn't tell the difference between the two [2]. Once children's voices are trained, there is no difference between girls and boys until they reach puberty. The differences in untrained voices are cultural, not physical (pp. 13–15).

9 'Children shouldn't sing difficult songs, their voices can't manage it'

All voices have limitations, regardless of age or sex. There are some difficult songs that can be sung by certain children, and some that can't. To simplify the classification, we can look at what makes a vocal task difficult. Because of the way in which the larynx works, anything that is high, loud, fast or long can be considered as a vocal extreme. By looking in more detail at voices at each stage of development, we can understand both the potential and the limits of the voice. With this knowledge we are better placed to decide what can be learnt and what can't (p.30, 49, 60 and 64).

10 'Cathedral choristers are more likely to get voice problems'

One would imagine that this is quite likely: these children are performing to high professional standards every day. This places them under high levels of vocal and emotional pressure. My own PhD research into choristers' vocal health showed that the opposite was in fact true, the choristers had healthier voices that any other group of children whom I assessed. It is likely that children under pressure can adapt: they develop strategies to limit the impact of the activity and preserve their singing voices (pp. 162–166).

These are just a few of the myths to be reinterpreted; there are many other examples of misperceptions in the way in which singing has been taught in the past. If we question these methods, this can make teachers uncomfortable. We all seek security in our belief systems; when these are challenged, emotions can run high. What we will actually find is that all of these ideas have arisen with the best possible intentions; the problems occur when they are misinterpreted.

The role of the singing teacher

Singing is only meaningful to the listener when the imagination is alight. Singing teachers have always used imagery to communicate ideas to the pupil and this is an excellent way to teach. In addition to a vivid imagination, however, the teacher needs to *really* understand what is happening vocally in the pupil. Imagination and intuition alone are not enough. The overall role of the singing teacher is as a facilitator: the teacher is using a combination of his or her skills in order to support a creative outcome. It may help to think of the teacher as having three equally important facets: **Intuition**, **Imagination** and **Information**. These legs of the three-legged stool are supporting the central act of **Creativity**.

How can a book tell anyone how to teach? Surely the skill of teaching can't be described in words? The skilled singing teacher combines practical experience gained from both teaching and performing with an intellectual knowledge of how voices develop and function. In common with all teachers you will need communication skills, empathy, a curiosity driving you to keep learning, personal organisation and, above all, enthusiasm. It's always risky trying to communicate the essence of good teaching with a book. There is already plenty of published scientific evidence on physical development, vocal technique, stages of learning and vocal health. This book does not prescribe a teaching method; it is a summary of relevant, research-based information that has been tried and tested in the teaching studio. If you like, it is providing more for the 'information' leg of the three-legged, creativity stool. The other two legs can be strengthened from other sources. My aim is to act as a catalyst to stimulate ideas, whether you are new to teaching singing, or have been doing it for years.

New to teaching?

Teachers who have trained primarily as keyboard players, conductors or classroom teachers often coach young singers. Despite their own extensive experience of working with children, these teachers may not themselves have sung at an advanced level. They may not have much knowledge of how voices work or of children's vocal development. Having said that, there are numerous inspiring and effective teachers who base their practice largely on intuition which is, as we have seen, an essential ingredient in a good teacher. I am hoping that this book may provide some additional information to enhance the knowledge and practice of experienced teachers, as well as inspiring newer teachers.

Many people will have had their learning environment clouded by a culture of fear, failure and guilt. This may come from within the individual, from those in their peer group, or from teachers. Pupils will generally undervalue their ability: they may cover their insecurity with a veneer of confidence and ambition, but this is often only superficial. Singers need kind, empathetic nurturing during their training and throughout their performing life. They need permission to fail: making mistakes and learning from them takes courage, and it can only take place if the pupil feels safe to do so. If lessons are seen as places for serious play, you and the pupil can enjoy the act of exploration. The teacher can create space for the singer to grow, suggesting goals without shattering dreams.

Chapter 1

Why sing and why teach singing to children?

'Use what talents you possess: the woods would be very silent if no birds sang there except those that sang the best'. Henry Van Dyke (1852–1933)

1.1 What is singing?

Darwin suggested that singing evolved before speaking as the main means of human communication. This is a compelling idea and there is now more recent evidence to support it [3]. This theory suggests that early communication was most effective using sung sound. Raw emotive vocal gestures such as wailing, calling, laughing, shrieking and sobbing are much closer to singing than to speech. Because of these emotional roots, singing has the power to move us. With or without words, we can understand the emotional message on an intuitive level.

1

Darwin suggested that singing evolved before speaking....

The voice is a means of communication among many mammals. Barking, roaring and crying are all ways of attracting the attention of other animals, whether they are friend or foe. All mammals can communicate aggression, fear or sexual intent with their voices. Humans, however, possess a unique alignment of the larynx (voice box) within the vocal tract (throat) that enables them to access a much wider variety of sound qualities than any other animal. These sounds are varied and subtle; they have enabled humans to evolve speech and song as an integral part of their social existence in every culture around the world.

The art and craft of singing can be sub-divided into at least four parts.

Communication

Singing is an emotional outpouring. Whatever the context, there is a mood, a response, a message to convey. This may be within a performance situation, where one singer or group of singers is presenting a vocal item for the entertainment and pleasure of an audience. As a group activity, singing forms part of rituals within society: religious ceremonies, celebrations of key events in life or socially bonding activities. In all of these, singing is used as a way to share a feeling; emotion is at the core of it all.

Musicianship

This includes aural skills, reading skills, musical memory skills and improvisation skills, as well as a more detailed understanding of musical structure and musical style. For a solo singer, this involves the interpretation of a song: dynamics and phrasing at the micro level (the relationships and inflections of individual notes within a phrase), at the macro level (overall musical shape, hierarchical relationship of phrases within that shape) and at a contextual level, establishing the song against a background of history and culture. For a choral or group singer, musicianship also covers balance and blend between singers and between parts. Musicianship can and should be on both an intuitive and an analytical level. Analysis is useful in the learning and preparation of the music. Intuition and instinct, which can develop as a result of exposure to the style, or from the analytical process, are vital for conveying integrity and meaning in performance.

Technique

This is the learnt muscular coordination of the breathing mechanism, the larynx and the vocal tract. It permits control of **pitch, loudness,** vocal **timbre, onset** and phrase length. Technique can help text to be articulated clearly without compromising the musical line. It is also vital for maintaining stamina and regulating pacing throughout rehearsal and performance.

Technique is vital for understanding
stamina and pacing.....

3

Learning a technique enables the singer to have a more efficient way in which to use his voice. It allows the singer to be more in control of the voice, so that he can express his musicianship and interpretation.

Repertoire

Most singers will want to learn to sing a variety of musical styles. Vocal repertoire can include music from diverse cultures and historical periods. Singers may learn to sing in languages other than their native one and are often required to sing about subjects that may not have a direct relevance to their own experience. The knowledge and acquisition of repertoire is enriching for every singer.

Put simply, singing is musical expression using the voice.

1.2 Singing is good for your mental and physical health

There is much evidence to suggest that musical activities have quantifiable benefits for children's education and development [4]. On one level, this should be considered as nothing more than an interesting by-product. Singing should be valued in its own right: it is an enormously enjoyable social, physical and spiritual activity. Satisfying our primal need for emotional communication is arguably a more important justification for singing than whether it helps the child achieve higher grades in literacy or numeracy. However, we know that all music teachers have to function in environments with limited resources, whether these are financial restrictions or limits on the available time. It may be useful, now and then, to have some empirical evidence at hand to influence higher management decisions. For example, quoting the wider benefits of singing could help to swing an argument in favour of keeping a choir going, or funding a specialist music teacher within a junior or elementary school.

Recently there has been more research on the effect of music on the brain and specifically, on brain development. In the 1990s there was some suggestion that listening to Mozart enhanced the individual's problem-solving ability and this became known as the 'Mozart effect'. On further investigation this proved to be nothing more than the consequence of listening to arousing music rather than either calming music or sitting in silence. It was further demonstrated that the music of the group Blur

All music teachers have to function in environments with limited resources...

was even more effective than Mozart. Listening to music can have short-term benefits to our mental state; this can be either for arousal or calming. We recognise the influence of music every time we make a choice of what we listen to.

As well as the known benefits of music education for improving overall academic achievement, recent studies have shown that singing in particular has a positive influence on health and well-being [5, 6]. The enhanced emotions generated can have a positive effect on the immune system over time [7].

The significant improvements noted in the research into academic achievement for children were as a result of music training over a period of time. It would appear that there is a direct causal link related to the acquisition of **fine-motor skills**, memorisation abilities, the expression of emotion and the rewards of group activity [8]. So it's not enough just to put your child to bed with a recording of Bach as background; if you would like your child to benefit from the effects of music on the brain, she will need to engage in musical activities. Luckily, singing is cheap (no need for instruments) and accessible (everyone can have a go).

The national 'Sing Up' programme launched in the UK in 2007 has resulted in measurable positive outcomes for children and their teachers [9]. The aim was to develop a national singing programme for junior schools, which has been done by promoting singing as a cross-curricular

Music is good for you!

tool and by providing training opportunities for teachers. Evaluation of the project after four years showed significant benefits for the children who were participating: a greater improvement in their singing abilities, and also in their self-esteem and sense of social inclusion [9].

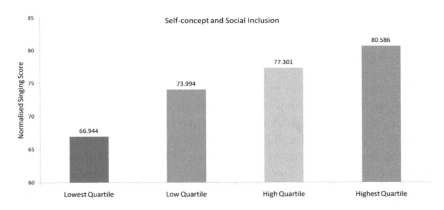

Figure 1.1: This shows the direct relationship between children's self-concept and sense of social inclusion, and their singing ability. The horizontal axis shows the values for social inclusion and self-concept, with the lowest quartile containing the children with the lowest self-concept. There is a direct correlation between the confidence and sociability of the children and their singing ability. The better singers are more confident socially [10].

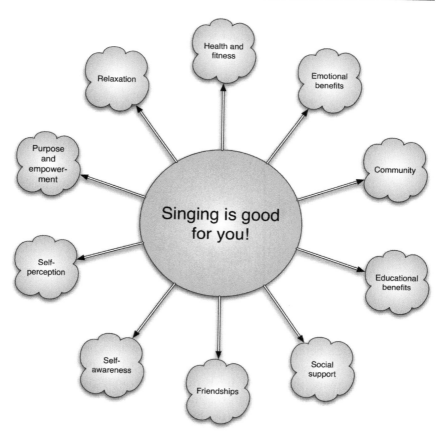

Figure 1.2: Some of the advantages gained from singing.

1.3 Why do children need to learn vocal technique?

There is an often-used argument that singing is a 'natural' activity; that all children can do it and that over-attention to the mechanics can take away the spontaneity of singing. It's true that everyone who can speak can sing, in the same way that everyone who can walk can dance, and that everyone with hands and arms can bang a drum. It is also true that some awareness of body use, muscular coordination and structured practice can improve the performance of every singer, dancer and drummer. So, absolutely everyone can sing to some extent, and yet everyone could learn to sing better. No one can be a great singer without education, experience and practice.

What is 'safe' technique?

The first issue here, especially with children's voices, is the idea of 'safe' singing. A prime responsibility of the teacher is to make sure that the singing activity should not be harmful. This applies in the short term (voice tiring, voice loss), in the medium term (the acquisition of bad habits), and in the long term (the healthy development of the voice into adulthood). In fact, nearly all of the advice in this book relating to appropriate vocal technique will also apply to adult singers; the 'safety' aspect is no different. In essence, safe singing is efficient singing, efficient singing is easy singing. We shall see, as we progress though this book, that the young singer is able to learn a great deal of technique that is in fact applicable to singers of all ages. The limitations for young voices are mainly to do with more extreme vocal gestures: these tend to be ones that are high, loud, fast or long. In other words, younger singers should avoid extended singing on high pitches, or singing too loudly, or passages of fast notes, or singing long phrases, or any combination of the four.

Technique means efficiency. This is the case with any physical skill, whether playing tennis, dancing, kicking a football, playing the violin, skiing or singing. Efficiency is using the minimum of effort to perform the task; the muscles can work at their optimum without interference from unnecessary use. It should follow that learning singing technique

Efficiency is using the minimum of effort to perform the task.....

will make it easier to sing. If we agree that we can learn to perform a task using as little effort as possible, we now need to define and understand the nature of the task. This will involve learning new skills and strategies as well as developing stamina.

It would be ideal if we all knew instinctively how to use our bodies and voices in the most effective way. To some extent this is true; we tend to use our voices very well when we make instinctive primal noises such as sighing, laughing, crying or wailing. The key here is that these sounds are emotionally engaged. The impulse for these emotional utterances is controlled by the limbic system; this comes from the more primitive area of the brain. The limbic system is a set of brain structures involved in many of our emotions and motivations, especially those concerned with survival. As well as connecting directly to our emotions, this nervous system is also responsible for controlling the muscles of the larynx. When we make uninhibited emotive noises, we are generally using our vocal system as efficiently and effectively as we can. The problem comes when we try to make the link to performing a piece of pre-determined music. We have to incorporate and direct our primitive emotive sounds into the words and notes of a song. When we are singing, all too often we are thinking intellectually, trying hard and over-working. Learning singing technique can help to combine the two types of brain activity.

Celia

I was watching this young singer of about 21 years old, going through the motions of singing 'Amazing Grace'. She was in tune, accurate, her words were clear, her breath sustained well to the end of each phrase. There was nothing actually wrong with her rendition; it was just boring and uninspiring. To be fair, she had been asked to do this, just to sing it correctly but without connecting to any feeling at all. Then, she was asked to think about certain images in her head; the song of the slaves on board the ships to the US in the eighteenth century, the power and meaning in the single word 'grace'. There was absolutely no technical instruction, no suggestion of rubato, of ornamentation, of types of onset or phrasing. As each new idea was added, she had pictures, feelings, sounds, emotions, colours and moods all superimposed, piled up on each other. The effect on her performance was extraordinary. Celia moved the audience of 120 people to tears. An analysis of the differences between the technical and musical interpretation of the first version and the final one would have shown a huge amount of detail. This type of instruction was not necessary though; just feeling the right emotions was enough to lift an accurate song into something sublime. This is not an argument against studying technique; Celia was an experienced performer with years of study behind her. The fact was, she had absorbed and embodied her technique to the extent that she had a direct connection between an emotional idea and her vocal performance. It's what we all aspire to!

The techniques of singing are about achieving balance; some areas will be working relatively hard while others will have to learn to let go. Much of the time, learning to sing is about learning where and how to release. Often, singers work harder than they need to and this tends to be counter-productive for good singing. If the singer is able to understand the concept of the isolation of effort, he can learn where to engage and where to relax.

The consequences of singing with inappropriate or harmful technique may be the development of voice disorders – these are not very common and are explained in more detail in Chapter 7. The other, more pernicious, issue is the development of bad habits, which will almost certainly lead to voice problems in later years. This is a much more common outcome and applies on some level to nearly everyone. However, just because we as adults may have learnt to overcome our early habits, it does not mean that it is acceptable for following generations to be neglected. Teachers have a responsibility to ensure that children in their care have the best possible input at an early stage.

Clare

Like most of the singers in her generation, there was no question of having singing lessons while at school in the 1970s. She began lessons when at university and continued throughout her further education and career. Clare had four teachers over a ten-year period, each one highly respected at conservatoire level. She was a professional solo singer for many years, working in opera, oratorio and recitals. Then in her early 30s technical problems began to dominate and undermine her singing. She was having problems with singing flat on certain vowels. She was beginning to lose stamina, becoming tired after only 10 to 15 minutes of singing. After consultations from a number of expert teachers as well as an assessment from a laryngologist, the diagnosis was unclear. Clare had muscle tension dysphonia, caused by anxiety, which was in turn caused by vocal unreliability, which had at its root some almost imperceptible technical faults.

Following on from the diagnosis of muscle tension dysphonia, Clare came to me to study. Then came the process of deconstructing her singing habits in order to regain her performing ability.

At the age of 18, Clare had realised that the 'really good' singers around her all sang with vibrato. So she copied them and added a wobble; this was subtle and sounded about right, but it involved some tension in her larynx and tongue root. Later, as a postgraduate student, she was asked to sing with a lower larynx, and without knowing how to do this, she pressed down with the already tense root of her tongue. She made a rich mezzo sound and was very successful for several years until the trouble set in.

> It took us about a year of regular lessons in which we went through the systematic re-learning of her technique. The voice that she discovered was actually richer and fuller than it had ever been. Most importantly, it was a voice that was able to perform reliably again.

This story is not unusual; most singers have some bad habits. Some habits are just more stealthy and underhand than others, in the way in which they can systematically demolish a singer. Some singers emerge stronger and wiser after vocal problems; some never manage to find their way back onto the career rollercoaster.

How do children train to become high achievers in physical activities?

If we want to look for evidence for or against the teaching of singing technique to children we find that there is hardly any information on this subject. Thinking laterally, other areas of technical training for children will include sports and dance. There has been scientific research into these areas and we can draw parallels with singing training. Any person training to perform a physical activity to a high level of achievement will be stretching the capabilities and limitations of their body. Whether it is gymnastics, piano playing, swimming, ballet, choral singing, football, musical theatre performing, skateboarding or rugby, there is a link. The key here is that in sports training we know that **the acquisition of an appropriate technique is essential in order to prevent injury** [11].

This fact is central to all athletic and dance training in children so why should singers be any different? We would not consider teaching advanced ballet to a child who had not undergone rigorous and lengthy training in how to use his body correctly. We would not expect a child to be able to swim 100m freestyle in under one minute unless she had been coached in a precise and detailed way. This training process has at its core the learning of the right technique. It is essential if we want to achieve an efficient and balanced physical performance. As teachers, if we don't do this, or we get it wrong, then at best the performer is not achieving his optimum in the skill; at worst he may suffer injury. In fact, it could be argued that any expectation of high levels of performance from a child without appropriate coaching in technique could be seen as neglect or even exploitation.

1.4 Differences between girls and boys

The subject of gender differences in singing is an interesting and yet controversial one. Boys will normally score worse than girls in pitch accuracy as well as in their self-perception as singers. However, at least in the UK, there is a tradition that the 'elite' child singers, those in the cathedral foundations, are boys. This could be that boys' ability is more polarised, with boys inhabiting the extremes of both excellence and incompetence. However, more recent research has suggested that any differences are due to culture not aptitude [12].

The boys will always seem to lag behind....

There is very little physiological difference between boys' and girls' vocal apparatus pre-puberty. There is, however, evidence to suggest that boys and girls will adopt a manner of speaking which identifies with the male and female adults around them [13]. Men have a larger larynx and a longer vocal tract than women, giving them a lower speaking pitch and lower overtones in their voices. To an extent this difference can be imitated by lowering the larynx and lowering the pitch (or vice versa) – we all do this action instinctively when imitating either a deep male voice or a small child. From an evolutionary and anthropological point of view, a deeper voice indicates a larger and therefore more dominant individual. A higher voice will by contrast indicate a more submissive individual. In very general terms, boys will speak with a slightly lower pitch and slightly rounded lips (lengthening the vocal tract), whereas girls will speak with a slightly higher pitch and more of a smile in the sound (pulling back the corners of the lips shortens the vocal tract – p. 102). These differences are very subtle, but enable listeners to identify accurately the sex of a child speaker, despite the fact that boys and girls have an almost identical vocal apparatus. This has been shown when expert listeners were played recordings of children's voices [2]. Younger children's voices were more easily confused, with more of them being labelled as girls, regardless of their owner's gender. By school age, the differences between boys' and girls' speaking voices were more accurately judged by the listeners.

The difference comes when the children are trained to sing. Some listeners claim that the sound of a boys' choir cannot be matched by that of a mixed or a girls' choir. From the age of 10 to the onset of puberty, boys do have a slightly larger larynx than girls. However, in a trial, even experts could not differentiate between recordings of a boys' choir and a girls' choir, both of which had been trained by the same conductor [14]. In trials using solo singing voices, listeners tended to confuse gender and age. Young boys were thought to sound like girls, older boys and girls were nearly always identified correctly but trained girls were thought to sound like boys. There is more information in later chapters on the gender differences with in-tune singing at different stages of vocal development (p. 48).

Encouraging boys to sing and then maintaining their interest throughout school has always been a challenge. Although there have always been more male composers and conductors, in Western culture boys and men have participated in less musical activities than women and girls [15]. To encourage more engagement with music, it is important that boys have positive role models, both in their own age group and in adult men around them. Music making for males needs to be physical; boys will tend to choose instruments that they perceive as needing strength and energy: drums, brass, cello/bass or rock guitar. Singing will be chosen if it is loud, active and in a large group. Critical mass is crucial: if most boys are seen to be singing, they will all want to join in. Singing cannot be seen as an activity for the 'musically gifted' or effeminate. It is equally important that sports and music are not placed in direct competition with each other. Boys should be able to play football as well as sing in the choir.

14

It can help if boys and girls sing in separate choirs between the ages of about 8 and 15. Beyond this age, the boys will be developing their adult vocal range and will not be in any sort of competition or comparison with the girls.

Chapter 1 Summary

- It is likely that singing evolved before speech.
- When learning to sing, we are working on four main skill areas, communication, musicianship, technique and repertoire.
- Singing has been shown to increase feelings of well-being and to improve self-esteem and social skills.
- Participating in musical activities can improve literacy and numeracy skills, the acquisition of fine motor skills and memorisation abilities.
- Learning a singing technique, at any age, not only can enhance performance but also can reduce the risk of vocal strain. Learning technique is making it easier.
- Boys' and girls' voices (pre-puberty) do not differ noticeably in structure although they may use their voices differently.
- The gender of trained children's singing voices cannot be distinguished with any accuracy.
- Boys tend to lag behind girls, both in their ability to sing in tune and in their enthusiasm for singing.
- It is important to give boys the right motivation to sing.

Interlude A

Singing in tune

The fact that some people, both children and adults, have difficulty singing a song in tune with others can be a source of great anxiety and unhappiness. Many adults will relate stories about traumatic experiences at school, where they had insulting comments made by teachers and were told not to sing. Teachers, in general, are much more sensitive to this issue now, and will try to enable the less confident singer to participate.

Sandra

Sandra was in her mid-40s when she came for lessons. She had been for an audition with the local choral society and had been rejected for singing out of tune. Her desire was to pass the audition next time around. She had a strong voice, but her pitching was random and rarely even near accurate. The first thing I told her was that this was not my specialist area; that I could give her one lesson and then we'd find a suitable teacher for her. However, I soon realised that I liked her attitude and admired her approach to learning. She was fun to work with and very eager to learn. We explored together and she worked diligently from the recordings of her lessons. She had these on her MP3 player and sang along to them whilst walking the dog every morning. Initially in lessons I focused on my voice tuning in with hers rather than asking her to tune with me. She learnt to feel when our pitches matched. She learned simple pentatonic sequences of notes. After six or seven lessons her naturally strong voice had found its confidence in tuning. The choral society was not the right place for her (too stuffy, too much emphasis on sight-reading); she got a place in the chorus of the local operatic society and hasn't looked back!

Singing in tune is a progressively learned skill: no child is born able to sing in tune, all children need to learn it and they all take varying amounts of time and input to achieve it. In order to sing a note at the same pitch as a heard note, the brain has to hear the pitch and send a message to the muscles of the larynx. The muscles have to know the exact configuration to produce a note of that pitch and voice it without delay. The process is complex, like throwing and catching a ball. The term 'pitch-inaccurate singer' is much more appropriate than 'out-of-tune', or even worse, 'tone deaf' which is generally an incorrect description. Pitch inaccuracy as a result of a hearing impairment occurs in only a tiny minority of individuals. The most likely reason for inaccurate pitch-matching is a lack of exposure to music in early childhood [16]. Another common cause is a lack of confidence, often as a result of unfavourable comments from other children or adults. Development of inner hearing and the muscular coordination necessary for vocal pitch matching is variable between individuals, much as is the development of speech, reading, ball skills etc. Some children are pitch accurate at the age of 2, others develop this skill at the age of 8, most children are somewhere in the middle and will develop mostly accurate pitching at the age of 5 or 6.

Singing out of tune?

The development of 'inner hearing' or audiation is crucial for singing in tune. The development of kinaesthetic awareness is also essential. This includes the physical feeling of tuning in, or matching the vibrations (frequency) of the other singers. Anything which can link aural, kinaesthetic and visual stimuli can be used; this may be simple hand gestures showing pitch contours, or using hand gestures for the notes on a scale (do, re, mi etc.). This system, linking hand gestures to the degrees of the scale, was initially used by John Curwen in the late nineteenth century. The system was then further developed by Zoltán Kodály in Hungary in the early twentieth century. If the child and teacher both use hand gestures as they sing, the child has both visual and kinaesthetic stimuli alongside the aural one.

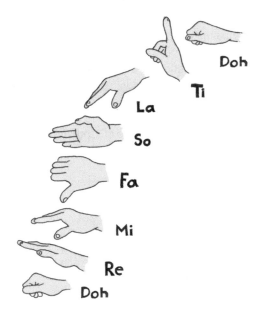

Figure A1: The Kodály/Curwen hand signs are made with the hand in front of the body. The low 'doh' is at waist level, each rising pitch is then placed slightly higher with the high 'doh' at eye level.

When working with the pitch-inaccurate singer, it is useful to remember that fragments of melody without words are much easier than complete songs. The singing of text may encourage the child to revert to speech-like sounds that have more limited pitching, whereas using non-verbal phrases enables the child to focus on the sound alone.

It is important to consider where in the group to place the inaccurate singer. It can sometimes help to put the individual in the middle of the group or next to more accurate singers. However, the inaccurate singer placed in a large group may just opt out and not tune into or take responsibility for his own individual sound. Also, if the singer cannot hear herself because the noise in the immediate surroundings is too loud, she will not be able to make adjustments as a result of auditory feedback. Some space between singers in a group singing situation is always helpful [17].

When offering individual help to the singer, it is worth noting that a piano is only a suitable acoustic model for children who are confident at pitch matching. If the child is asked to pitch the same note as a piano, or another instrument, the acoustic properties of the sound can be confusing to someone who is not used to isolating the pitch element from the timbre. The child may be puzzled by the vast array of overtones, some of which could appear to be stronger than the fundamental pitch. Any musical instrument will have its own timbre, or distribution of overtones. The human voice, used at the same pitch as the child, will be the best guide. It can help if the teacher tunes in with what the child is singing, rather than asking the child to tune in with the teacher. This enables them to gain kinaesthetic as well as aural awareness of tuning in. Ask the child to sing a note, or a fragment of melody, and sing along with the child at his pitch. Use visual gestures for up and down.

Modelling can be an issue if the teacher is an adult male with a singing voice an octave below the children. It is accepted now that in the early stages of singing development, the child finds it easier to sing if the adult teacher sings in falsetto at the same pitch as the child, even if the quality of the singing from the adult is not as comfortable. As singing becomes more confident, it is then advantageous for the male teacher to switch to the more comfortable lower octave. The child will be able to make the aural transposition of an octave relatively easily, and will find the vocal comfort of the teacher a more useful model.

Most school classrooms now have computer facilities; software which gives a visual representation of the pitch is readily available. This can be a very useful aid, especially with the singer who is only slightly inaccurate [18]. For example, the tuning of notes in a descending scale is nearly always lower than those in the ascending scale. This is the case for even a skilled singer, and it is sometimes easier to see this on a display than it is to hear the difference.

Chapter 2

Children from birth to 6 years

'Education is not filling a bucket, but lighting a fire.' W B Yeats (1865–1939)

2.1 The musical experience of the unborn baby

The developing foetus hears sounds both from within the mother's body and from outside. Due to the filtering effect of the amniotic fluid, sounds at a frequency above 300Hz are altered; this includes some music and the voices of children. Adult voices and low frequency noises are not altered as much. Internal sounds are much louder to the foetus; these include the mother's voice, heartbeat and intestinal gurgling. We know that a baby in the uterus can respond to sounds, as the baby's heartbeat can be measured. This will alter, either by slowing down or by speeding up, depending on the nature of the sound or music.

The foetus is also sensitive to hormones from the maternal blood. They will be generated as the mother's response to basic emotional situations. These will include those caused by anxiety or fear as well as positive responses which come from social contact or singing. These hormones will be transferred to the baby who will learn to associate certain audible signals with emotional responses. An appropriate emotional response to certain situations is therefore already in place at birth. There are evolutionary benefits to developing such a response to sound pre-birth. The newborn infant will not only be able to recognise its mother's voice, but it will be able to judge the tone of her voice. The baby will know that an anxious tone denotes a threatening situation and that a calming tone signifies a safe environment. This communication from the outset is essential to ensure survival.

There is conflicting information on the value of musical experiences for the foetus [19]. Now that we know that a baby in utero will respond to and possibly benefit from exposure to music, we would be justified in thinking that playing music to a baby would be beneficial for its emotional and musical development. It could be tempting to play music via speakers placed directly on the mother's abdomen in order to stimulate the baby's musical development. There are several reasons, however, why this is not a good idea. It is quite likely that music that is too loud (especially with low-frequency sounds such as drumbeats) could potentially damage the hearing of the baby. It is also worth remembering that a baby in the uterus will have a pattern of waking and sleeping that is not necessarily the same as the mother's. Too much loud noise at the wrong time of day for the foetal sleeping pattern could be disruptive for the baby's general development.

It could be tempting to play music directly on the mother's abdomen... this is not a good idea.

The key here is that the musical experience of the foetus needs to mirror that of the mother. If the mother is listening to or participating in some music making, her 'happy hormones' will be telling the baby that it is a good thing. It is now accepted that musical experiences enjoyed by the mother will give positive messages to the baby. The mother's health and well-being is paramount to foetal development: if she is enjoying musical experiences, the developing baby will benefit from this.

2.2 Early singing, carer and infant

The first vocalising a baby does is crying. This in itself contains all the elements of singing: pitch contour, varied rhythmic intensity, loud and soft, and most importantly, emotional communication. After a few weeks, the child begins to coo and then babble. Babbling will contain prosodic features and speech fragments of the mother tongue: French infants babble with French **phonemes**, Japanese infants with Japanese ones.

The baby's carer will instinctively speak to the baby in a generally higher pitch range with extended vowels and a greater pitch variation. This is known as 'motherese' and contains all the musical elements of song. All cultures have infant-specific songs, for both calming and stimulating the baby. Singing is nearly always accompanied by physical movement; again, this can be rocking for calming the baby, or jiggling movements accompanying stimulating songs. This intuitive behaviour between adult and child will develop musical activity as an integral part of the child's environment.

2.3 Musical and language development

Infants' hearing and perception of music is surprisingly sophisticated. At the age of 6 to 10 months they can recognise familiar tunes even though they may be played in different keys. This means that the contour of the tune itself is familiar, not just the physical sensation of the particular frequencies. Babies can also recognise changes within familiar tunes [20]. They respond strongly to pitch contour, which is an integral part of speech prosody. Infants respond more favourably to consonant intervals (e.g. the perfect 5th) rather than dissonant ones (e.g. the diminished 5th). They can also readily discern metrical structure, remembering whether music is in rhythmic units of two or three beats. All of these attributes are cross-cultural; they appear to be genetically programmed in the human from the outset.

For the young child, one of the most impressive learning achievements is that of learning to speak. When this process is examined further, some general patterns of behaviour emerge from the teacher (parents or carers) and the child.

- The child can observe the tangible benefits of the use of speech in the world around him. He is immersed in a speaking environment from the outset.
- Speech is observed and copied, rather than being taught.
- Early attempts at speech get a positive response; even approximations are rewarded.
- Incorrect responses are generally ignored rather than criticised.
- The child chooses the rate at which to try out new words and to practise familiar ones.
- The learning environment is supportive and non-threatening.

Learning to speak happens when the child is young enough for the brain functions to be adaptable; the areas of the infant brain responsible for specific tasks seem to be interchangeable, to an extent, up to the age of 4 or 5. It is much easier for children to learn a language fluently and with accurate pronunciation if it is started by this age. The same flexibility is seen in the brain patterns of young children's musical activity. Whereas adults tend to exhibit stronger left-brain activity for rhythmic features and right-brain activity for melodic ones, the infant and young child show plasticity and flexibility in the processing of musical features.

2.4 Musical play

All children use singing in their play. This may be a free-flowing string of sounds often used in solitary play, or when singing to toys. It can be vocal sounds illustrating movement or activity, a sort of 'comic-strip' vocalising. These voiced sounds may accompany play with objects such as toy vehicles, play weapons or toy animals. Children in kindergarten, for example, will also use repetitive chanting in play with each other. This may be known songs or just be based on fragments of songs. The pitch range used for this spontaneous vocalising is often small, up to a fifth at this age. This will be the same pitch range as they use for speech.

All children use singing in their play ...

2.5 Educational development

All research related to educational development states the importance of musical activity in the early years. There are many schemes and publications giving a potential musical framework for every part of the school day: songs for taking coats off, songs for lining up, songs for 'circle time', songs for being quiet and listening and so on. Once the children know the songs, the teacher merely begins the tune, the children join in as it catches on and the activity follows on. How much nicer that is than shouting for attention! It is also possible to use songs for literacy, songs for numeracy as well as songs for exploring other ideas such as moral dilemmas. Songs integrated with movement will have greater impact and be more easily memorable. Although songs with a purpose are important for educational development, there is also the possibility to sing songs just for fun!

2.6 Physical development

The vocal structure of the infant

An understanding of the voice of the newborn baby is crucial to our understanding of the changes that occur later. This is down to the basic fact that the voice of the infant is fundamentally different from that of the child, adolescent and adult. The baby is not born with a miniature version of the adult vocal system; it has its own particular and specific needs from the voice, larynx and lungs, which are unique to the newborn, immobile, vulnerable, human infant.

To put it simply, infant vocal structure is based on the survival requirements for crying and feeding. The child and adult vocal structure is based on the requirements of speaking and running.

First, the height of the larynx in the neck is different. If you feel your own larynx, it sits about one third to half of the way down the front of the neck. The infant larynx sits right up behind the jaw. The main benefit of this raised position is a feeding advantage. At the top of the larynx is a cartilaginous flap, the epiglottis. This is part of the swallowing mechanism; it closes over the top of the larynx to protect the windpipe as food passes into the oesophagus. In the infant, the high position of the epiglottis allows it to overlap with the soft palate, enabling simultaneous sucking and breathing. You can watch a baby feeding in this way: it takes two or three sucks, and then it swallows. The seal formed by the link between the epiglottis and the soft palate enables the baby to fill the mouth completely before swallowing. This is a much more effective and faster way for the baby to fill up its stomach with milk – an important advantage for the rapidly growing baby.

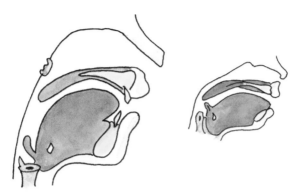

Figure 2.1: The position of the larynx (coloured blue) in the adult (left) and child (right).

The illustration shows the relative height of the larynx in an infant and an adult. In the infant, the larynx is level with the jaw. The adult larynx can be felt situated mid-way down the neck. Another advantage of the high larynx is that it is much more effective as an anti-choking protection. The lower larynx found in adults is not so effective as a valve; this can cause difficulties in old age when swallowing problems may become an issue.

A disadvantage of the high larynx is that the range of vocal colours is relatively small. A shorter vocal tract (the tube from the vocal folds to the lips) limits the opportunities for a varied vocal timbre, including forming different vowels. This is not a problem for attracting attention (crying loudly) or for experimental burbling; it would, however, be a problem for speaking. One could say that the trade-off for evolving a mechanism suited to speech is the potential to choke!

It is tempting to use the crying of a baby as a positive example of efficient sound production and seemingly endless vocal stamina. On further examination, it appears that the model is actually very different and can't really be compared with the vocalising of children and adults. An infant's lungs are proportionately smaller and the ribs are more horizontally positioned than those of the adult. This allows room for a proportionally larger digestive tract; it is absolutely crucial to the baby that it gets adequate nutrition for growth and development. Horizontal ribs are not as mobile as the hooped ribs of the adult; consequently all breathing in the infant is done using the diaphragm only. Babies breathe with abdominal movement (using the diaphragm to inhale) because they have no option – they are unable to use the intercostal muscles to move the ribs.

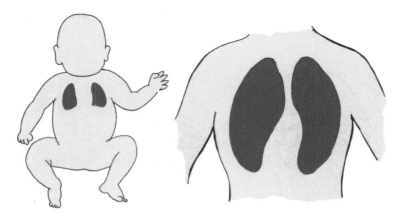

Figure 2.2: Relative lung size of infant (left) and adult (right).

Children and adults have bigger lungs and use a combination of diaphragmatic and intercostal movement. This means that they can utter longer phrases, necessary for speech. They can also get more air in and out, which is crucial for athletic activity such as running. Babies have no need of the type of deep and extended breathing needed for either athletic activity or speech. Their need is to attract the attention of the adult who may feed them, by making as much noise as possible.

The infant needs to have a constantly high respiratory rate in order to maintain its rapid growth and development. Despite its small lungs, this is achieved by having a breathing rate of about 80 breaths per minute (and adult breathes between 12 and 20 times a minute when at rest). The difference is that the infant cannot significantly increase its breathing rate whereas the child and adult can. The main reasons for needing a marked increase in lung capacity are due to the demands of more extreme physical activity such as running, and extended vocalisations such as speech. Neither of these apply to the infant, as it is not physically active enough to need larger exchanges of oxygen and carbon dioxide and is also not yet using speech. The voicings of the infant are no longer than two or three seconds at a time, whereas connected speech requires at least five-second vocalisations.

In addition to this, the sound babies produce is very penetrating: the high, small larynx can produce and enhance high frequencies in the sound, which grab our attention. The crying sound, although it has the essence of singing sounds within it, is rather limited if one compares it with the variety of colours in any style of singing or in speech. We can see that infants have a very different vocal set-up from children and adults, and that direct comparisons are of limited use.

The vocal structure of the young child

The specific vocal set-up of the infant gradually develops to that of the adult: and it is this shifting which gives the young voice many of its recognisable qualities and also limitations. The survival requirements of the infant are clearly based around attracting attention and getting food. As the child becomes more mobile, basic yelling is still useful as a means of communication, but so is the development of speech. The desire to learn to speak is partly driven by the frustration the child feels at being unable to communicate. Their language comprehension is always ahead of their speaking ability. By the age of 3 or 4, a child's survival is far more dependent on its ability to be able to articulate its needs using language. It is essential, therefore, that the vocal mechanism adapts to enable this.

To allow this shift for the development of speech, the larynx descends, the laryngeal cartilages become more firm and mobile, and lung volume increases. As the infant matures, the lungs move into a vertical position, and by the age of about 8 they assume an adult-like structure when sounds of a longer duration become possible. This is a gradual process and continues through puberty and beyond. The lungs of the child are still relatively small and they do not permit extended sung phrases.

The laryngeal cartilages are still relatively soft and movement between them is still comparatively clumsy. Because the cartilages are more compact in relation to each other, there is less room for manoeuvre. The practical implication of this is that pitch range is reduced and that rapid pitch changes are more difficult (young children don't tend to sing coloratura passages). The vocal fold structure is relatively thinner and with a less well defined layering of tissues. The amount that the vocal fold can move with each cycle, or the vibration amplitude, is less: this restricts the possibility of a large dynamic range. Due to the relatively clumsy relationship of the muscles and cartilages, young singers have a limited ability to increase intensity without impacting intonation. As they get louder, they tend to get sharper in pitch.

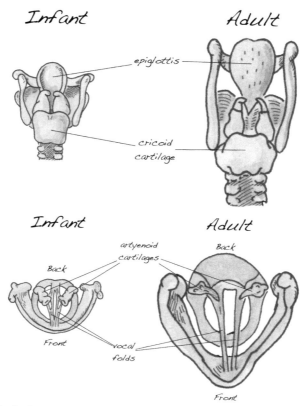

Infant   Adult

epiglottis

cricoid
cartilage

Infant   Adult

artyenoid
cartilages   Back

Back

Front   vocal
folds

Front

Figure 2.3: *The developing larynx.*

The vocal tract is still short. Although the position of the larynx is descending relative to the neck or the cervical vertebrae, this can't happen overnight and as a process takes several years. The seven cervical vertebrae, or bones of the neck, are a useful marker for larynx height. The infant has a larynx level with C3, the adult larynx is level with C6 or 7. Children are somewhere in between these two. Within the vocal tract are all the resonant properties of the voice. A high larynx means a short vocal tract, which restricts, to some extent, fullness of vocal resonance (p. 102).

An adult can imitate the timbre of a young voice by speaking with a raised larynx. The higher overtones produced as a result are not to be confused with higher pitches. The adult larynx can be raised and lowered whilst speaking on the same pitch (it takes a bit of practice to do this). The timbre of a young voice is recognisable; during a phone call we can immediately identify the approximate age of the child on the other end. This is because a younger child has a higher larynx, with a correspondingly short vocal tract. An articulate 5-year-old will have a different vocal timbre from an 8-year-old, even if the pitch of the voice is similar.

2.7 Singing technique: what can and can't be done

Children of this age (birth to 6) will not be able to learn technique as we might consider it. They may not have the muscular awareness and coordination consciously to control individual muscular activities. They can, however, learn good habits for later. In general the child singer has a reduced capacity for vocalisations that are disproportionately long, agile, loud, high or rich in timbre.

Posture

Encourage the children to stand for singing, even though they may get fidgety after a while. If they then move to sitting on chairs, you can encourage them to sit up, away from the back of the chair. If they are sitting on the floor, this can cause problems. It will encourage the back to round and the head to tip up and back, in order to raise the eyes to the level of a standing adult. It is best to vary the position between sitting and standing.

If you ask them to 'hold their heads up' they may well just put their chins into the air. Shorter children may be doing this anyway. Ask them to 'stand up straight like soldiers' and they will stand stiffly. If you ask them to 'stand long and tall like a hanging puppet' they may loosen their arms and shoulders. A good way to ensure balanced body use during singing is by movement. Most children's songs for the pre-school age group are action songs. Movements linked with the words are helpful for memorisation as well as effective and balanced body use.

Breathing

This will be mostly an instinctive action at this stage. You can discourage 'big breaths' that they may be doing by lifting the ribcage. Draw their attention to their posture instead and the breathing will fall into place more easily.

Pitch range and voice timbre

Children can be encouraged to explore and use the upper pitch range; this may be between E4 and C5. It can often help them to sing all pitches more accurately as they move away from their habitual speaking pitch. It will also reduce the degree of vocal fold closure and make them less 'shouty' (p. 92). If they find this pitch range difficult to access, you can often help them with comic-strip noises. These are whooping, calling, wailing, mewing, buzzing, yelling, whining, hooting, cooing – work your way from the racetrack, through the farmyard, via the zoo, and into outer space.

By the age of 5 or 6, more musical children will be able to learn to sing rounds and canons. This is the beginning of part-singing.

Singing in tune

Children of this age will find it easier to sing a melody in tune if it doesn't have words to it. As children generally associate text with speaking, they are liable to adopt a speaking voice rather than a singing voice when encountering words, with a consequent lack of pitch accuracy [21].

Figure 2.4 shows the accuracy of children's delivery of the separate elements of song. These are the words alone, simple glides, musical fragments and whole songs.

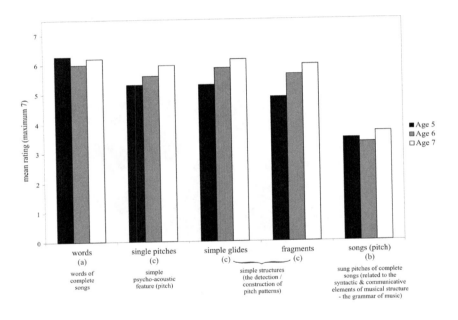

Figure 2.4: Longitudinal data on 5 to 7 year old children's rated singing abilities for (a) words alone of target songs; (b) sung pitches from the same complete songs; (c) deconstructed pitch elements from the songs [22].

If the pitch elements of a song are deconstructed into shorter fragments during the learning process, then young children's pitch accuracy is better. When approached in this way, there is no difference in pitch accuracy between boys and girls. If the song is presented as a whole, then boys are less accurate than girls.

2.8 The relationship between parents and teachers

If you can involve the parents at this stage, the more support that they give you the better the outcome for the child. If the parents know the songs being learnt they will hopefully sing them through with the child at home or on car journeys. The value of music in the home and for family life is another book altogether, but as teachers we can encourage it.

If the parents know the songs they can sing them on car journeys.

Chapter 2 Summary

Musical experience of the infant and young child:

- Musical experiences begin prenatally for the unborn baby.
- The sounds are associated with the hormonal input from the mother, whether these are threatening or pleasurable.
- 'Motherese' is often close to singing, babies learn to associate music with both calming and stimulating messages.
- The infant brain is very adaptable, this helps with the acquisition of speech.
- All children use singing, or non-speech vocalising as part of their play.
- Musical activities for the very young can help their educational development.

Vocal structure of the infant:

- The infant has smaller lungs (to enable more space for digesting food).
- The infant has a higher larynx (to limit choking and aid rapid feeding).
- The infant has a less mobile larynx (more effective as a valve, less effective for vocal variety).
- Infant vocal structure is based on the survival requirements for crying and feeding.
- Child and adult vocal structure is based on the requirements of speaking and running.

Establishing good habits for singing:

- Encourage good posture, tall and loose.
- Play with extending the pitch range.
- Encourage in-tune singing by using melodic fragments as well as whole songs.
- Young children have a higher pitch range than older children and women.
- Involve parents with singing activities as much as possible.

Interlude B

The learning process

Seven stages of learning

By dividing the learning process into stages, we can analyse not only our lesson structure, but also identify where something may have been missed out. If a stage has been rushed or skipped, the teacher may need to go back over it later. These seven stages are based on **psychomotor skill** educational theory [23]. In order to illustrate them, it may help if you consider the learning process a young child has to go through in order to be able to walk and then run. This begins with the child observing older people standing and walking, then wanting to reach for more interesting objects for which standing is necessary. The child tries a few steps and it is some time before these can be connected without the child falling over. In fact, learning to walk is just the process of learning to control the movement of falling over.

Consider the learning process a young child
has to go through to walk and then run.

Eventually, after much practice, the child can walk and then run. This relatively simple action will take over a year to achieve, with constant practice. Skilled (fast) running won't come for a few more years. It's a slow and steady process that, in the early stages especially, needs a great deal of help and encouragement.

The **first stage** is **pre-exposure** to present an overview and initiate the **desire to learn**. This is sometimes a difficult initial hurdle in the classroom situation. If the group dynamic is negative at the outset, then there is some persuading to do. There are many ways in which a teacher can motivate a group but peer pressure is a very powerful influence, however inspiring the teacher. Often the willingness to learn can come from exposure to role models, either from elsewhere in the school (older pupils who are seen to be 'cool' and who also love singing), or from outside. There has been some important outreach work in the UK recently that has involved taking cathedral choristers into primary schools. The singers met the other children, ate with them and played football with them. Once they had been accepted, they then sang to them and with them. The response was often a real change of perception for the children.

Report from Head Teacher: The schoolchildren were amazed that the choristers were as good at football as they were, and yet they could also sing to such a high level. This encouraged them to engage with the singing programme, which helped in turn to improve the children's interest in school in general.

Report from class teacher: Daniel and Joe both have Attention Deficit Disorder, needing 1:1 attention during normal school hours. They joined in with a singing session with the choristers and were fully engaged throughout, for the first time ever in the school.

So – assuming that you have your child or children wanting to learn how to sing, you can move on to the next stage.

The **second stage** to learning is **preparation**, for the singer this is starting with the right body and mind set-up. This includes mental, physical and emotional readiness. There should be the minimum of distractions, the singers should be standing or sitting with alert poise and mental focus. Giving attention to the task is surprisingly difficult for adults, let alone children. Get the child ready physically first; this can then sometimes help to 'remind' the intellectual and emotional states to join in and focus.

The **third stage** is **initiation and acquisition**. For this, demonstration and explanation from the teacher will be needed. This may include vocal exercises or the learning of phrases within a song. At this stage immersion in the activity is helpful, providing an overview and generating some curiosity in the student.

The **fourth stage** is **elaboration**. For the singing student this will generally mean the repetition of smaller elements such as exercises or phrases. It is essential in order to enable the muscular responses to become habitual, thus freeing the thought processes for imagination and improvisation. Repetition of technical exercises can be boring, but it can also be calming and the predictability can be reassuring. When the student has just got something right, ask him to do it again straight away. This may be frustrating for the student who wants to move on immediately but it is crucial for the **motor memory** aspect of learning. Get him used to the idea that repetition is part of the process: that it's always going to happen. Children will accept and often feel comfortable with repetition and ritual, especially if they know that there's a reason for it.

The **fifth stage** is **memory encoding** or the linking of smaller habitual units into larger bundles. These larger bundles are known as **automatisms**: they are direct paths for performing a task, without having to go consciously through all the stages in between. For example, a small habitual use may be the release of the belly for the in-breath (see p. 83). This can then be linked with the onset of the sound (at the right pitch and loudness) (see p. 96). With practice and repetition the in-breath will then automatically be followed by a particular onset. This gesture can then be linked with balanced posture (see p. 81), so that as the sound is initiated by the breath, the posture remains stable and directed upwards. This can then be linked with the breath control needed to sustain the particular phrase (see p. 87) – and so on. If these detailed aspects of technique are habitually performed at the same time, the singer can

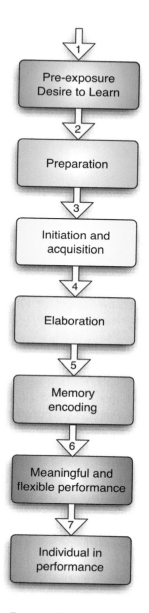

Figure B1: The seven stages of the learning process.

eventually begin to 'sing' and these actions will all be switched on simultaneously, without any conscious direction from the singer. This is the point at which the brain processing has become embedded in the cerebellum, the habitual action site. The more that these pathways and groups of actions are repeated and rehearsed, the easier and quicker it becomes to perform them automatically. Returning to the image of the child learning to walk, this would be the stage where the child can stand up and walk over to an object without faltering. The only way to get to this stage is repetition and practice.

The **sixth stage** is the assimilation of all this into a **meaningful and flexible performance**. This means working with extended phrases, whole run-throughs, exploring the emotional journey of the piece, trying to uncover the true meaning of the text and finding the emotional reason for every musical gesture. For our child learning to walk, this may be the discovery of jumping, skipping and hopping.

The **seventh stage** is the freedom and flexibility to be **individual in interpretation** and performance. To witness the student achieve this is always the ultimate goal of any music teacher. Again, returning to the image of the child learning to walk – if we consider this stage to be that of skilled running, there is a long way to go between walking without falling over, and running 100m in under 20 seconds. These seven stages are not of equal length or importance but they are all essential in the learning journey.

Motivation

Motivation is linked to self-concept and the perception of ability. Young children can have a very general but often inaccurate concept of what they are particularly good at. They will tend to generalise with blanket statements about their abilities. By the age of 9 or 10, children have a domain-specific and more accurate self-awareness. They may say, for example 'I'm really good at running, fairly good at maths and really useless at spelling'. Instilling confidence in the child is crucial for every aspect of her development. As teachers, we also need to balance this with some realistic and positive awareness of how far the child has to go and how she is going to get there.

We know that a child will achieve most if he has a realistic self-concept. The issue for the teacher is one of flexibility, balancing expectations so that the child is not over- or under-challenged. Children are often labelled in an educational environment as having particular ability levels: they may be considered to be high, average or low achievers. This categorisation may help the teachers to have the right sort of expectations; it also helps the grouping of children according to ability within a class or year group. However, it may not really help the child in the long term, as it does not take into account individual differences of understanding and learning. This fixed ability concept not only limits the child to a particular set of expectations, it also suggests that these labels can only be altered when the child outperforms other individuals in set tasks. It is often the case that the factors enabling change are external: the potential to change is therefore outside the direct control of the child. In contrast to this, a child with a malleable ability concept has some control over her progress; for example, she may aim to improve a specific skill such as singing at sight. The child with the malleable ability concept will be more successful than the child with the fixed ability concept [24].

This idea can be simplified if we think in terms of dreams and goals. A **dream** is personal and private. The pupil may have completely unrealistic dreams, or they may be redefined at stages in his development. It is not the place of the teacher to question or to undermine dreams. A **goal**, however, can be proposed by the teacher or by the pupil. It is essential that goals are realistic and achievable, even if they may appear to be challenging.

Motivation to keep trying, despite possible failures, is based primarily on the way in which the student perceives the outcomes of her actions. Maintaining a realistic self-awareness in the student through appropriate appraisal and direction is generally in the hands of the teacher.

Robert

Robert was a young baritone with an exceptionally lovely voice. He was intelligent, charming and musical. However, he had started three different university courses and dropped out of each one after a year. Each time he had an important concert or audition, he would prepare for it, but would then do something stupid. This often involved drinking too much, sometimes it involved drugs. Everyone despaired of him. This became one of the main problems; Robert had too many people expecting him to do well. He had been led to believe that he was great and should be successful and yet he wasn't really sure about his own abilities. The drinking was just providing a get-out clause; he could blame the circumstances for his subsequent failure.

We worked slowly and steadily. Robert built up a more secure technique, he learnt what was and was not reliable. He began to notice patterns in his behaviour when under pressure. He prepared his repertoire meticulously; I gave him very detailed practice schedules that he generally managed to stick to. He slowly built up his inner confidence, based on tangible outcomes. There was a happy ending; he was awarded a scholarship to a good conservatoire and has remained there. I'm sure he's still a bit silly from time to time, but I suppose that's part of his charm!

Making mistakes

Making mistakes is a crucial part of the learning process, it can also be one of the most frustrating. When the pupil is learning something new, or even singing at sight, she will inevitably make a mistake at some point. You, the teacher, may stop her, point out the error and suggest that she does it again. Very often the pupil will just repeat the same mistake. This can be simply due to the way that the brain accesses information when in a new situation. If the brain is searching for the right note, it will inevitably grasp a familiar note. This will probably be the wrong one the pupil has just sung. In order to bypass this, suggest that the pupil sings a wrong or just different note at this point. The brain has been released from latching onto the familiar and will take the next best option – this is likely to be the right note. Once this is done, repeat this with a linked sensation or idea. This can be a feeling, emotion, technical idea or an image. The pupil can then use this link to have instant access to the right note each time (see multi-sensory learning pp. 181–182). This approach can be used for any repeated mistake, not just wrong notes. It is important to give the pupil permission to go wrong. If he is concerned with accuracy at all times, he will never take a risk. It is only by taking a risk that singers can change and develop.

Types of intelligence

Howard Gardner [25] outlined nine types of intelligence: these are not fixed, they are all teachable and all interdependent. They are also all applicable to musical study. Each individual has a balance of ability and aptitude in each of the nine areas of intelligence. If the teacher can recognise the particular strengths of the individual, these can be used to help develop the weaker areas.

- Musical – the link is self-evident, although there may be children who have a beautiful or a strong voice who may not be musically intelligent.
- Linguistic – learning and understanding song text, often in different languages, critical analysis of music, understanding historical context.
- Logico-mathematical – reading rhythms, structural analysis of music.
- Spatial – structural analysis and composition, reading notation on a score.
- Bodily/kinaesthetic – learning and performance of technical skills, performance choreography.
- Interpersonal – communication with an audience, working with other musicians, teaching music.
- Intrapersonal – understanding emotions, self-awareness of strengths and weaknesses, and performance anxieties.
- Spiritual/existential – possibly involved with the emotional and aesthetic aspects of music.

- Naturalist – understanding of the materials within musical instruments, how they work and interact; how musical instruments interact with each other, families of instruments; to have a similar understanding of the body and how it creates sound.

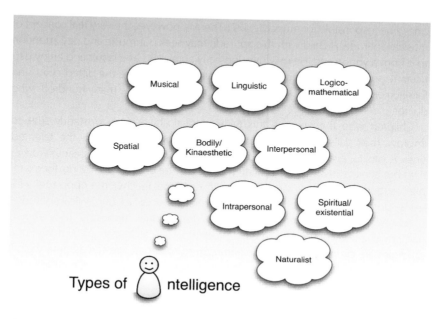

Figure B2: Different types of intelligence.

There are numerous links and crossovers between these intelligences. Gardner suggests that the more of these links that are made, the more successful the individual becomes. As each one of the nine intelligences can be linked to an aspect of music making, this would add to the argument that engaging with music is a life-enhancing activity, one of comprehensive educational benefit.

What is 'gifted and talented'?

The use of these terms is one that has generated heated debate among educationalists. There is a common misperception among both children and adults that musical ability is something innate. When asked in a general survey, the only group of people who did not believe this were musicians and music educators; they understood the role of personal investment and the learning environment [26]. Comments after a performance such as 'you are so lucky, being able to …' although meant well, can often undervalue the years of study. This attitude only arises because nearly everyone would love to be able to play a musical instrument or sing well. Outstanding ability in artistic areas such as dance, fine art and music seem to fall under a blanket of chance elitism; as opposed to sporting achievements which are generally recognised to be the product of years of specialist training.

There is some disagreement between experts on whether there may be a specific gene responsible for musicality [27]. There is, however, the very real concept of musical aptitude. A child with this aptitude may seek out music and pay attention to it from a young age. He may develop early aural skills as a result and enjoy particularly positive rewards from musical activities. This may be the 'gifted' child, and for each one who goes on to succeed in music, there may be many hundreds who do not.

Children who then pursue this early musical ability and constantly seek to improve their skills with realistic challenges and goals are possibly the 'talented' ones. Again, for every one of these children, there are many who appear to work as hard but achieve less. For such children there may be one factor missing: for example, a supportive home environment, an inspirational teacher, the opportunity for extra-curricular musical activities, self-esteem or simply a lack of physical aptitude.

So the 'gifted and talented' emerge as exceptional musicians. They should not, however, be confused with child prodigies, such as Mozart or Menuhin; true prodigies are extremely rare. In the nature/nurture debate we can assume that all humans are innately musical. Although some individuals have more aptitude than others, the nurture aspect has far more influence on musical outcomes in the individual. There is evidence to support the idea that a minimum amount of study is necessary before an individual can achieve expert skills in any area. Examples might include dance, chess, football, computer programming, piano playing, music composition or painting. The necessary amount of study in which to achieve expertise has been suggested to be approximately 10 years, although some sources suggest that 10,000 hours is more accurate [28].

There is a common pattern among all high-achieving individuals. When interviewed, world-class pianists have said things like 'When I was 6 or 7, I did very little practice, maybe only an hour a day'. We may find this level of commitment at such a young age surprising, whereas the pianist views this as completely normal. This possibly obsessive interest in the activity at a young age will be recognised and encouraged by the parents. In the childhood years, parental support is crucial. For instrumental players, the parents attend lessons and supervise daily practice. Parents will often have made huge sacrifices, both personally and financially, in order to give their child the best opportunities. During teenage years, the individual will practise for many hours a day, every day, regardless of other distractions. Alongside this, there is a level of skilled teaching and teaching support that is crucial for the individual. This level of commitment is a very rare thing; chance and luck are an element of it, yet consistent hard work is the common factor.

Within the pop industry different factors are involved. Much hard work is commonly put in by producers, publicists, stylists and sound engineers to mould the raw material into a commercially polished 'package'. In the world of pop music, stars have often been created out of people who have never done much studying or practice. With the lack of voice projection needed in pop, it is possible for the singer to learn the art form in a relatively short space of time, much more quickly than classical voice. The requirement to have a good voice may be lower on the list of priorities for being a pop star, and there are those who make it big with a less than adequate vocal ability. There are of course, true vocal athletes in the pop industry, for example, Beyoncé. There are also many who have had sustained career success, some shining examples would be Shirley Bassey and Tony Bennett.

Chapter 3

Children aged 7 to 12 years

3.1 Context

Singing is an integral part of play at this age; this is generally observed more in girls but not exclusively so. Playground songs are chant-like; you will see children singing while clapping, skipping or making other types of movement. If you observe closely, you can see that some of the clapping songs have very complex cross-rhythms and syncopation; these sophisticated patterns can be developed and passed around the group. The tunes are, as with the younger age group, generally limited to a fifth, although the range can be as much as an octave. Favoured intervals are minor thirds, major and minor seconds. As well as their own songs, children can be very inventive with parody songs. These use the structure and tune of familiar songs but with the children's own words.

In a more formalised context, children in this age group may be singing in a wide variety of situations. Group singing takes place in school, church, community and rock choirs, theatre or dance school ensembles and many others. Solo singing opportunities may arise from one of these groups, or through talent shows, festivals or graded music exams.

At this age, children are capable of learning specific muscular coordination, that is they can learn certain ways of using their bodies to enable more effective singing. In the group context, some basic technique is useful. Children can learn good posture, basic breathing patterns and a variety of voice qualities. In the solo singing context, technical guidance is valuable if they are to perform at their best. This is the ideal age at which to begin some good habit-forming; once learned correctly, these habits can be useful for the rest of the individual's singing life.

As a teacher, we should never underestimate the impact that we may have on developing minds and voices. The longer-term benefits of a good basic grounding in vocal technique and musicianship are immeasurable and very rewarding.

James and Oliver

These two boys were cathedral choristers taught by me between the ages of 8 and 13, although they were a couple of years apart from each other in the school. They were both very good singers and were each busy with a lot of international solo work in their last year or two at the school. Singing at this level was very rewarding. They worked hard, practising every day and having extra singing lessons to manage the workload. When it came to voice change, however, they were both grateful for the opportunity to focus on other music making. At this point they had moved schools and therefore moved on to other teachers. Both of them stayed in touch, and they came to sing to me now and then in the holidays. The reason I mention these two in particular is because eventually they both went on to sing professionally. They have both told me, on separate occasions, that their singing technique learned as choristers kept them going for years afterwards, and is still important to them now. They had enough knowledge and awareness from their early training to work out any problems for themselves later as they went along. Education can't be taken away!

3.2 Physical development

The physical development of the voice and body during this stage is one of gradual growth. There are no sudden or dramatic changes; the related structures such as the lungs increase in size and the larynx lowers slightly. The most noticeable differences are those of coordination and control. These include both fine control (for example, holding a pencil and writing) and gross motor skills (throwing and catching a ball, riding a bicycle). From the age of 7 or 8 the child will be able to learn movements and gestures with increasing levels of complexity and skill. The larynx and the vocal folds will show some changes: these are in the layering of the vocal fold tissues. An infant vocal fold in cross-section will show basic differences between the muscle layer and the epithelium, or outer layer of mucosa. As the child grows, these layers become more defined. The epithelium shows three distinct layers and the vocal ligament can now be shown as starting to develop. This runs the length of the vocal fold and provides tensile strength, especially at higher pitches. The structure of the vocal folds is described in more detail on pp. 90–92.

3.3 Musical development

Musical education can take many forms for this age group. It has been shown that participation and play are much more effective than instruction. Children's perception of sound does not necessarily fit with the adult European concept. Children will link musical experiences of loudness, rhythmic repetition and pitch contour to other sensory experiences.

The association of pitch contour with vertical positioning appears to be embedded in our subconscious mind. In experiments with both infants [29] and even with chimpanzees [30], it has been shown that audiovisual mapping is present at a basic level. Infants will associate vertically elevated images with higher pitches, and chimps have been shown to link brighter lights with higher pitches. These visual clues may be obvious, but when we use language to describe sounds, there may be confusion from the ambiguity of musical terms. Descriptions such as high and low can apply to pitch as well as loudness. Physical directions are confused with pitch directions. In order to make the pitch on a keyboard higher, you move to the right, rather than up. On a cello raising the pitch means moving the left hand downwards. Children can also be confused by the complex nature of a single sound; many percussion instruments have strong overtones as well as the noise of impact. Descriptions such as fast and slow could apply to the overall length or the rhythmic tempo.

If they are given the opportunity, children can be inventive and descriptive with whatever sounds they have at their disposal. Musical composition can be made relevant across the curriculum. Singing is a highly versatile musical sound available to all children.

Reading musical notation

There are conflicting arguments regarding the value of teaching musical notation. Some teachers advocate aural learning before reading, others teach both skills simultaneously; there is, of course, value in both approaches. The child learns to speak long before learning to read or write; the aural skills are assimilated before the visual decoding skills are addressed. This is also an important element of musicianship: singers need an inner hearing before they can make sense of written notation.

The other side of the argument is that children learn to speak their mother tongue (or tongues if they are multilingual) in infancy, but they tend to study music and further languages after the age of 5 or 6. The process within the brain by which they acquire language as infants is flexible, but becomes more fixed by the time they start school (p. 23). By this stage, the learning process within the brain has altered, and reading skills can be learnt alongside aural ones. If, however, as is often the case in instrumental tuition, reading skills are taught without aural skills, the child will become a 'button pusher'. When sight-reading music, the notes will have become symbolic for physical actions on the instrument, rather than as connected sounds. This is another strong case for all instrumentalists to learn to sight-sing.

Certain musical cultures do not rely on written notation: the repertoire is learnt entirely through listening. With singing and song learning within the Western Classical culture, reading from the musical score is not necessary until the child is singing at a more sophisticated level (part-singing in choirs, learning solo songs). Nevertheless, for healthy brain development in all aspects of music making within this culture, it is arguably the case that children should learn to link the written notation with the sound of the music. This is easiest if done from the outset, albeit at a basic level.

3.4 Singing in tune

In general, boys are less accurate with pitch matching. This is the case for all ages. Although boys' pitching will improve as they get older, so will that of the girls, so the boys will always seem to lag behind.

Boys, when asked, will often say that they are less good at singing than girls: singing tends to be considered by both girls and boys to be a girls' activity. One solution to this is to have separate boys' and girls' choirs for children. Although this separation can be considered to be socially unfavourable, if it gets boys to sing, the advantages may outweigh the disadvantages. The three-year programme 'Sing Up', in UK schools from 2007–2010, showed the impact of regular singing upon children's singing abilities. In those schools participating in the programme, all the children, regardless of gender, showed significant improvement in their singing skills [9].

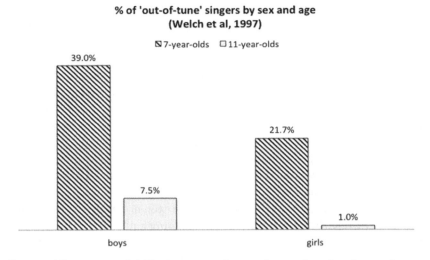

Figure 3.1: The percentage of children singing out of tune at the ages of 7 and 11, showing the difference between boys and girls at each age [31].

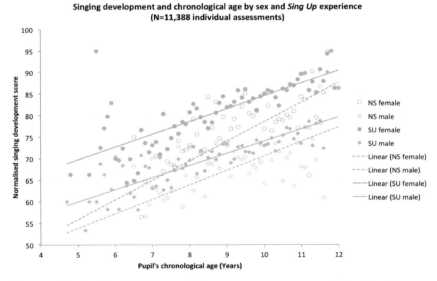

Figure 3.2: Graph to show the development of singing accuracy over time, in both girls and boys, with (SU) and without (NS) a structured singing programme [32]. Although the NS (dotted lines) children made progress with their singing over time, the SU (solid lines) children had a higher level of singing development throughout the study.

If they are in a school which fosters and encourages singing at all levels and in all situations, children will have more advanced and confident singing skills. This, in turn, will lead to more confident social skills, improved numeracy, literacy and self-esteem.

3.5 Singing technique: what can and can't be done

This is the age when children can begin to learn effective breathing technique, related to balanced posture. This is explained further in Chapter 5. They can also learn different voice qualities and choose between them appropriately. The limits at this age are still, to an extent, pitch range, loudness, flexibility and stamina.

Pitch extends downwards a little as the larynx grows and the speaking voice lowers. Pitch extends upwards depending on the individual. Some singers manage to sing up to C6 and beyond. Many children will find it less comfortable to sing in their upper range. This is not surprising, as it requires greater flexibility and practice. A higher range can be encouraged with the use of non-singing 'noises', such as whooping, wailing, sighing, and so on as described on p. 31. These intuitive noises also tend to be made with low connected breathing.

0 - 2 yrs   4 yrs   6 yrs   8 yrs   11 yrs

Key: x = speech F$_0$, • = speech range, o = singing range.

Figure 3.3: Pitch ranges of children in speaking and singing (based on [33] and [10]).

The pitch ranges show:

- *Extended singing range* (unfilled note). This is the pitch range possible with no observable sign of strain and without using falsetto.
- *Comfortable modal singing range or extended speaking range* (filled note).
- *Speech fundamental frequency* (cross). This is the average pitch for the child's speaking voice. It is usually three to four semitones above the lowest comfortable singing pitch.

Loudness is limited by the size of the larynx and vocal tract. This may be hard to believe if you are in a school dining room at lunchtime, but it is not appropriate to expect children to match the levels of professional adult singers. They are also not able to sustain loud singing or high singing for as long as adults. It can help if young singers think of dynamic levels as moods or colours, rather than levels of loudness.

This limitation of **stamina** is useful to remember if the children are singing repertoire written for adult singers. Most choral repertoire is written for adult voices. Children will need to be able to sing more quietly, occasionally sing down the octave and have more frequent breaks. If they are singing solo repertoire written for adult voices, they will need more frequent breaths, and will probably sing at a slightly faster tempo.

Since their voices are not as **flexible** as adult voices, rapid pitch changes are not as easy for them to achieve. This pretty well rules out long coloratura passages for all except the most advanced students.

Repertoire

All of these limitations are important when considering repertoire for children of this age. There are now many more publications and anthologies of songs specifically selected for this age group.

If children of this age are singing in groups, their technical skills can be dealt with in a more general way. If they are to perform at a higher level, for example in professional choirs or theatre ensembles, or as soloists, it is best that they have the right guidance from an expert singing teacher. Without this, it is inevitable that they will use their voices less efficiently. It is also likely that they will acquire bad habits that will need to be unlearnt at a later date. Children of this age who sing regularly not only develop their singing voice and their upper pitch range, they fare better in self-confidence and social skills. There is a linear relationship between improvement in singing development, children's self-concept and their sense of social inclusion. This is shown in Figure 1.1, p. 6.

3.6 The relationship between parents and teachers

The value of parental support for music activities in the pre-teen years is known to be hugely important. If at all possible, encourage parents to sit in on lessons and to supervise practice. Involve them in the experience and they will be able to help the child in ways that you as the teacher are not able to; this in turn will make the teacher's job much easier. Very occasionally it is clear that the child sees his singing lesson time as a welcome relief from pushy or dominating parents. In this case, you can try some lessons with parents and some without. However overbearing they appear, their opinions need to be imaginatively accommodated.

However overbearing they appear

Chapter 3 Summary

- Singing is an integral part of play.
- Play songs can be sophisticated and complex.
- At this age the child can learn more specific physical skills, breathing technique, extending upper pitch range and exploring different voice qualities.
- Participation and play are more effective than instruction.
- The involvement of parents is advantageous.

Musical development:

- Children have an innate sense of audiovisual mapping for music notation, this can become confused by ambiguous instructions.
- Learn musicianship holistically: combine aural, visual and kineasthetic. In other words, singing involves listening and reading notation as well as performing.
- Boys lag behind girls with singing in tune and also with their self-perception as singers. Regular singing can improve both aspects.

Singing abilities:

- Pitch range tends to be fixed at the lower end and extendable at the upper end. Range may be limited due to the size of the larynx.
- Loudness is limited also by the size and proportions of the larynx.
- Vocal stamina is not as strong as in older children, this age group will need more frequent breaks and less vocally demanding repertoire.

Interlude C

The child as a professional singer

There are enormous benefits to be gained by a child from the experience of professional solo singing. To be given the status normally given to adults with years of previous experience, to be trusted with that level of responsibility, to explore the detailed process of analysis and interpretation, to perform in large international venues, to attain an outstanding level of artistic achievement, to have VIP treatment, to be part of a greater musical experience, to do something that no one else in your school class is doing, maybe to have a tangible outcome – a CD or DVD. How special is that?

Professionally performing children with whom I've worked have inevitably reached a higher level of emotional maturity, reliability and musicianship as a result of the experience.

There are problems or potential dangers arising from giving a child the responsibility of high-level solo performance. For an adult, this experience would normally come after years of training and apprenticeship. An adult singer will be aware of the need for adequate preparation, will arrange (and pay for) all the necessary lessons and coaching, will have the experience to know how long this will take and how to pace the whole process. An adult is aware of his or her responsibility towards other performers, how to behave in rehearsal and how to present in performance. A child has to learn this very fast, and will have to be guided through every stage by someone with relevant experience of performing in this field as well as having empathy with the child. The teacher/coach/chaperone has to liaise with the conductor, other performers, wardrobe, lighting and publicity to ensure that the best interests of the child performer are being looked after. There is the legal side too: there are very strict guidelines on the working hours for children. I have often had to warn a conductor who may be 'on a roll' that we will have to break in ten minutes. The minute-by-minute management of the situation can be like treading on eggshells.

In terms of teaching and preparation, it is essential to know how a child's voice can be trained and what the physiological possibilities and limits are. It is important for the child to know that there is someone he knows and trusts, someone who can encourage him to go as far as he is capable but who will know when to say enough is enough.

If you have a pupil performing in a professional musical theatre production they may have to sign a contract that forbids them from working on their repertoire with

Ben

Ben was asked to sing the role of Miles in a professional performance of *The Turn of The Screw*. He was a cathedral chorister, an experienced soloist and a confident individual. I taught him the role but left the opera music staff to supervise his singing for the rehearsal period. They assured me that they knew what to do: the conductor was an ex-chorister himself. When I went to a performance I was horrified when I heard what he was doing with his voice. He had been encouraged to take his speech register as high as he could, essentially shouting the entire role.

He had one year left in the cathedral choir, but he never sang well again as a treble. I suspect that he had developed vocal fold pathology as a result of the opera, although this was never followed up. Happily, he is now a fine baritone and there are no long-term negative consequences. However, at the time I vowed never to be so trusting again!

any other teacher. This is to ensure consistency within and between performances. If your pupil is still coming for singing lessons during the rehearsal and performance period of the production, it is easy to monitor their vocal habits with exercises and other repertoire. If she sounds as if she is being encouraged to push or shout in the production, this will be evident as vocal tiredness, croakiness or hoarseness. You can always ask the child to demonstrate what she is asked to do in the production, without 'working on it'. If there is cause for concern, a message to the music staff via a parent should help.

There is a huge gulf between the world of high-art classical music performing and recording and that of media-featured entertainment. The long-term consequences of prolonged media exposure are probably going to be troublesome. It is very difficult to melt away into anonymity after such publicity, both for the child and for his or her peer group at school. These problems must be anticipated and handled very carefully by the parents, school and the child. I've never known the passage back into 'normal' life to be entirely trouble-free. It's part of the price, and hopefully the cost is not as great as the return.

The most important outcome should be that it is an enjoyable and rewarding experience for the child. If he's not having fun, then it's up to me to sort it out. Any teacher at times may have to take encouragement into the realms of nagging, or may have to say 'no' to the offer of a late-night party before an important working day. However, when it all goes well, and it generally does, then the rewards are absolutely fantastic. If one can assist this sort of enjoyment and excitement for a child, by ensuring that all aspects of work and play are carefully balanced, then everything is worth it.

Chapter 4

Adolescents

'The teacher sets a process in motion, rather than imposing it. The teacher's role is to instruct the student in the art of self-correction, of analysing and thinking, taking decisions, then applying them to the task in hand. The teacher's ultimate aim is for the student to become independent – to become a master rather than a pupil ... the teacher must be both.' Yehudi Menuhin

4.1 Context

Adolescence and early adulthood is a crucial period of development for defining musical tastes. One would think that teenagers would choose their social groups based on the type of activities in which they are most involved. Those in the school football team would hang out with footballers, those in the orchestra would hang out with musicians. In fact, in terms of social grouping, adolescents are drawn to groups with similar musical tastes more than those with common activities such as sport [34]. It is music that is the dominant influence for social bonding. The importance of our musical tastes during adolescence is reflected as we get older. Throughout their lives, nearly all adults favour music that was popular at the time when they were between the ages of 14 and 21.

The value of musical play in younger children is often obvious; in adolescents this is less so. This does not mean that it has disappeared. Instead of playground songs, teenagers will listen to recordings of songs within their social group. They will sing along and improvise dance moves; this is merely a progressive stage of the playground singing and dancing, and is a precursor to young adult activities such as clubbing and parties.

The influence of music in the teenage years is potentially huge: teenagers listen to an average of two and a half hours of music per day (*New York Times*, 13 February 2008). The messages contained within the lyrics can be alarming. The following troublesome themes may be prominent:

- advocating and glamorising abuse of drugs and alcohol
- racism and sexism
- pictures and explicit lyrics presenting suicide as an 'alternative' or 'solution'
- graphic violence
- preoccupation with the occult; songs about Satanism and human sacrifice, and the apparent enactment of these rituals in concerts
- sex that focuses on controlling sadism, masochism, incest, devaluing women and violence toward women.

Most teenage listening goes on out of earshot of parents.

Certain styles such as rap will contain more violent subject themes than styles such as pop or rock. Most teenage listening goes on out of earshot of parents or teachers. In general, a happy and healthy teenager will have no undue emotional problems whichever style he immerses himself in. Those who need to be watched are those who show signs of isolation, depression, or alcohol or drug abuse.

4.2 Singing technique: why teach it?

If adolescent pupils are to sing solo repertoire, it is important that they are taught appropriate vocal technique. Again, we are often up against the old idea that singing is 'natural' and doesn't need to be taught. This is not the accepted practice for any other musical performance skill. For example, if the child plays the keyboard or the guitar without guidance, she may manage to achieve a certain level. It is perfectly possible to learn to strum some chords or copy some guitar licks from recordings. In fact, many highly successful artists have managed without any formal tuition. But does this mean that it is the best way to go about it? We tend to assume that any kid learning to play a guitar will undoubtedly fare better with a few lessons. If the child has spent a great deal of time with unsupervised technique, this will often mean a return to simple exercises and a great deal of time spent unlearning bad habits. If children sing using their 'natural' ability without expert guidance, they will inevitably develop unhelpful habits which will either limit their future development, or have to be unlearnt before they can progress. It's not the end of the world, but it is better if it can be avoided.

4.3 Onset of puberty

Over the last 50 years the average age of onset of puberty has been observed to be falling worldwide. In 1950, the average age of onset was 14 for boys and 12 for girls [35]. Recent research suggests that the age of onset is nearer to 12.5 years for boys and 10 years for girls [36]. This is a drop in age of a year or two at most. There is no evidence to suggest that this trend towards even earlier puberty will continue.

There are five basic hypotheses for this phenomenon [37]. It is unlikely that any of them will be proved either right or wrong, although some are more likely than others. In general, this trend has been observed globally: it is not culture-specific.

- **Improved diet:** this could be the case, although some research suggests that diets were healthier in the 1940s and 1950s in the developed world than they are now.
- **Warmer climate:** although this refers to overall global warming, this would not explain why children from warmer countries reach puberty at the same time as those from colder climates.

- **Hormones in water supplies or beauty products:** this is possible, but we would expect early pubertal onset to be more evident in heavily populated areas.
- **Increased psychosexual stimulation:** this is exposure to adult images and expectations, and is a plausible theory.
- **Increased overall exposure to light:** without artificial light, the total hours of daylight over a 12-month period are the same for any location on the planet. In the last 50 years we have exposed ourselves to many more hours of light during our lifetimes due to the use of artificial lighting. This may have, to some extent, accelerated our growth patterns.

Duration of puberty can last from as little as eight months to over four years. Physical growth in general is in spurts or stages; a height gain is followed by a period of stabilisation. This growth pattern is caused by hormonal levels and cannot normally be accelerated or decelerated except by artificial hormonal input.

Delay to puberty can, however, be caused by severe malnutrition or severe emotional deprivation. It has been suggested that extreme physical exercise, as has been observed in some child dancers and gymnasts, could delay puberty. More recent literature suggests that the children and the body types for these activities are actually self-selecting [38]. Children who are smaller, slimmer and who may have a later onset of puberty are more likely to choose to be dancers or gymnasts, rather than the activity itself causing these tendencies. Changes to the onset of puberty have been observed in obese children: recent research suggests that obese girls are more likely to have early pubertal onset, but that obese boys are more likely to have delayed pubertal onset. This is due to the retention of small amounts of oestrogen in fat cells. In a normal healthy individual puberty is an unstoppable process.

During the pubertal growth spurt, the lungs approach adult size and vital capacity. However, adult vital capacity and total lung volume can only be estimated to occur by the age of 18 to 20, generally two to three years after the end of the pubertal growth spurt. Likewise, the height of the larynx does not drop to the adult position until the age of about 20. As the larynx grows in size in both boys and girls, the muscles within the larynx also grow. As muscles grow, they increase in length before they increase in strength. This means that immediately after a growth spurt, the muscles will be at their least coordinated.

 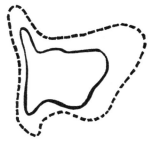

Figure 4.1 The relative size of the thyroid cartilage in the female (left) and the male (right), pre-puberty (solid line) and post-puberty (dotted line).

Although the vocal folds have essentially reached adult length at the end of puberty, the connective tissue of the vocal folds continues to increase in size and quantity into adulthood.

4.4 Adolescent girls

Physical development of the voice

The physical growth of the female larynx during puberty is relatively straightforward. The main noticeable change to voice quality can be an increase in **breathiness** or **roughness**. This is partly due to the way in which the **vocal folds** vibrate; growth will destabilise the existing pattern of vibration for a period of time. Girls also have a greater tendency to have a **posterior glottic chink** (see Breathiness pp. 97–98). This is caused by weaker **adductory muscles** at the back of the vocal folds and can be reduced or eliminated with technical exercises.

Girls' voices can also be affected by the onset of menses or the monthly cycle. In the few pre-menstrual days the vocal folds may become slightly swollen. This can lead to instabilities of pitch and voice quality. It can take several months for the cycle to settle into a more predictable pattern after the onset; during this time the girl may suffer vocally from increased breathiness, huskiness and pitching instabilities. In some girls and women, the discomfort and vocal unpredictability of their monthly cycle requires them to take a contraceptive pill. Research has shown that use of the low-dosage pill will reduce these unfavourable symptoms in the voice [39].

Technique: what the girl's voice can and can't do

At this age, the repertoire possibilities really begin to open out with the developing emotional and musical maturity of the singer. It is important to remember that the larynx is still young and potentially vulnerable. Adolescent girls still have limitations of vocal extremes: these are anything high, fast, loud or long. In general, repertoire written to be sung over a large orchestra is not suitable, even when sung with a piano. The phrases are long and expansive, there are more sustained higher pitches and the vocal timbre is generally fuller. Having said that, there is a wealth of repertoire which is suitable and which will facilitate the development of good, healthy and efficient singing technique. Apart from the development of louder, full-bodied vocal timbre, the technical possibilities for adolescent girls are not very different from those of young women who are five years older.

It is possible to develop and maintain effective and energised lower-abdominal breathing. Aspects of onset and sustain can be worked on, as can a variety of musical styles and their related vocal timbre.

Breathiness is often an issue, especially in the girl entering puberty. This can be worked on effectively; there are exercises for this in Chapter 5. Often the teenage girl will have a strong and well-developed lower range and a comparatively weak and breathy upper range. She will do anything to avoid singing high notes. There are many ways in which the balance for this can be redressed. First, sing more gently in the lower range, work on **deconstriction** and quiet singing in the lower pitches. Second, explore upper pitches with clear and energised sounds – these may be non-singing 'comic-strip noises' described on p. 31. This encourages resonant properties in the voice that can't be made with a breathy sound. Third, blur the boundary – bring the upper voice down beyond the pitch of the usual register change, give the singer options of different voice qualities on the same pitch. This movable register change is important to develop in all singers.

Singing high notes is an unusual sensation: it's not generally part of our everyday voice use. Girls may need to be encouraged to try it out; they may feel frightened that they will hurt their voices, or that they sound horrible or just weak and unable to project. Play with noises and have fun: the laughing pupil will learn more easily than the fearful one.

The laughing pupil will learn more
easily than the fearful one.

4.5 Adolescent boys

Physical development of the voice

Male vocal mutation through puberty is generally referred to as 'changing voice'. The term 'breaking voice' can be construed as a negative or destructive process. The term 'changing voice' is a more accurate description of the period of male adolescent voice mutation.

In boys, the thyroid cartilage grows primarily in the front-to-back direction, particularly at the very front tip, which forms the 'Adam's apple'. In girls, the thyroid cartilage growth remains more rounded. The male vocal folds undergo nearly twice the growth of those of the female: 65% increase in the male and 34% in the female. Within the larynx, the vocal folds of the boy increase in both length and thickness. This increased mass means that they vibrate at a lower frequency, hence the drop in speaking pitch.

Why has the adult male human evolved a speaking voice an octave lower than the female? The degree of growth (65%) is extreme, there must be an evolutionary benefit to this, and there are two possible theories. In many mammals the male of the species has a voice with either a lower pitch or with lower formants (p. 119). These voice characteristics will occur in larger individuals (a dog has a lower voice than a mouse). If the male is to intimidate an adversary or impress a female, it will be to his advantage to appear larger. Some animals (the red deer and the koala, for example) have the ability to lower the larynx dramatically as they call or bellow. This produces a sound that belies their actual size.

Another possible explanation for this much larger larynx could lie in the ability of the adult male to articulate clear text very loudly. Men have thicker as well as longer vocal folds in a longer vocal tract. This enables them to be louder for longer, it also enables them to have clear vowels at high pitches – this is not possible for women (p. 120). Perhaps in evolutionary terms, women were better off keeping their higher pitched voice to be 'in tune' with their children while the men evolved to shout at each other over large distances.

Men evolved to shout at each other over long distances.

Five distinct male adolescent stages of physical growth were clearly outlined by the paediatrician, James Tanner, in the 1960s. In the 1970s, John Cooksey assessed hundreds of boys' voices and recognised five stages of voice change. These physical and vocal changes have since been demonstrated to have a significant correlation with each other [40]. We know that voice change is directly related to physical growth. The maximum change in pitch occurs at the same time as the maximum growth, between stages III and IV. Although the pitch of the speaking voice is mainly dependent on vocal fold length, the sudden drop in pitch observed between stages III and IV is largely due to increased vocal fold mass rather than sudden elongation of the vocal folds. This can be heard as a significant change in voice quality as well as pitch.

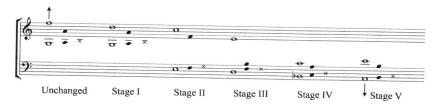

Key: x = speech F$_0$, • = speech range, o = singing range.

Figure 4.2: The pitch ranges of each stage of male voice change (based on [41] and [42]).

The pitch ranges show:

- *Extended singing range* (unfilled note). This is the pitch range possible with no observable sign of strain and without using falsetto.
- *Comfortable modal singing range* (filled note).
- *Speech fundamental frequency* (cross). This can be ascertained simply by asking the boy to count backwards from 20 and observe the pitch at which his voice settles most comfortably. This is usually three to four semitones above his lowest comfortable singing pitch.

Possible signs of change to Cooksey Stages I and II [41]

- growth spurt
- change of timbre in the mid-range of the singing voice
- decrease in control at the top of the singing range
- change in timbre of speaking voice
- increased variability; more 'off' days.

There tends to be more stability and less individual variation in the lower pitch range limit throughout the different stages of voice maturation than in the upper pitch range limit. Therefore, it is more reliable to judge the developmental stage by the lower singing range and by the fundamental frequency of speech.

Technique: what the boy's voice can and can't do

Assess the voice

The first thing that any teacher needs to do, when working with an adolescent boy, is to assess his voice stage. This is easily done by listening to him speak, preferably on a rather dull task such as reciting the months of the year, or counting backwards. He will settle on a sort of monotone. Hum along with him: you can do this an octave up if his speaking voice is too low for you. Then try the pitch out on a piano; it will be clear if the played pitch matches his average speaking pitch. If in doubt, keep repeating the exercise until you've got it right; it doesn't take long and it's extremely useful to know. You can then compare him with the stages on Cooksey's chart. Remember that these are based on averages, and that there will be many individual variations.

The move from Stage II to Stage III is not just indicated by a drop in pitch, you will also hear a change in voice quality as the vocal folds thicken. The voice will sound fuller or heavier. Boys are generally aware of their stage of vocal development, they can feel if it is different. They are also very good at noticing even subtle changes in the voices of their friends [43]. Ask the boy himself where he thinks his voice is.

Occasionally you may come across a boy whose lowest singing note is not a third below his speaking pitch. This may be because he is artificially lowering it (in order to sound older – common in the late developer) or raising it. Holding the speaking voice high can be done for several reasons if there is a tangible benefit to the boy. He may be trying to preserve his high singing voice in order to be able to go on tour with his choir, for example. He may be holding his voice high because he is uncomfortable with adolescent changes (see puberphonia later in this chapter). Whatever the reason for this, any pushing-down or pulling-up of the speaking pitch will result in excess and unnecessary tension in the system. It's not a good idea, especially if the boy is a singer, so try to get to the root of the issue and help him to sort it out.

So – assuming that you have a healthy boy with a voice somewhere on the way to a man's – what to do about his singing? The main thing to do is to trust your basic instinctive judgement: if he looks and sounds comfortable, he probably is. The ranges given by Cooksey are averages for all boys; you may find that the more experienced singer has a much more extended upper range throughout voice change. If the boy is in the early stages (I and II), then singing in the soprano range is still fine if it's comfortable. Once his speaking voice has lowered to G3 or F3, he is no longer a treble, but a developing baritone.

Should a boy continue to sing with his high pitch-range?

It's often tempting to let boys continue to sing high when their speaking voice is dropping. Boys with good vocal technique can often produce a strong and musical soprano range, even when their speaking voice would suggest a young baritone. This is because the larynx is still flexible at this point; the cartilages are growing rapidly but are still softer than adult larynx cartilages. The muscles carry on with their habitual use, even though they are growing much longer. The problem here is that the demands on the larynx become more and more extreme. If the boy continues to sing soprano during voice change, at some point the whole system will collapse and the boy can have a disastrous few months vocally, regardless of any potential problems later.

There has been research into this, in the USA, Germany, Sweden, Australia and in the UK [44]. The considerations have been for both short-term and long-term development. All of the research concludes that boys should not sing exclusively in the upper ranges during voice change. Notice that I refer to exclusive use of the upper range. Occasional use is fine; in fact it can encourage flexibility in the upper ranges. So it's not a problem for young tenors to sing some notes in falsetto. It's fine for all adolescent boys to use falsetto in their warming-up, and it is often an artistic requirement from time to time in pop or musical theatre singing. What is crucial is that the main body of the singing with a rapidly growing and vulnerable voice is within the fundamental comfort zone – as a tenor or baritone, at the lower end of the pitch range.

Another feature of the rapidly growing vocal system is a change in voice quality. The voice can be described as rough, thin, reedy, hooty or grating. It can become rich, full, warm, resonant or vibrant. These are all subjective terms and of limited use for accurate description, but they can give away a great deal about the expectations of either the boy or his parents. It is absolutely essential at this time that the boy is encouraged in his singing, that he feels excited by the possibilities opening up for him.

Stephen

Stephen was an extremely enthusiastic 14-year-old who bounded into his first ever singing lesson on a choral summer school. He'd always sung; school choirs, festivals, church choir and school shows. Not only that, but he thought he knew exactly what he was doing, because that's how he'd always done it and everybody liked it that way. He brought 'Where'er you walk' by Handel and sang it confidently in his soprano range. I was a little surprised; his speaking voice was centred around a D3, almost an octave below middle C. This could be tricky. I asked him about his comfortable vocal range. I asked him to try a bit of humming right down to the bottom of his speaking voice. We then tried some declamatory spoken words from the text of the song, and then played with pitching them higher and lower in his speaking voice. We played games without labelling or criticising anything. After about 10 minutes of this, I suggested a really silly game – let's try singing the song down an octave! Stephen was up for it, gave it a try and was utterly amazed. He became quite emotional and very excited. I suggested that he could try singing in the tenor section with the older boys, just to see what it felt like. He boldly strode back into the rehearsal and joined the tenors. He's now a professional tenor with one of the top opera companies in the UK. However, he still remembers and talks about that lesson, and how exciting it felt to sing with his full adult voice.

Most boys are thrilled by the prospect of developing an adult voice: this is an entirely healthy attitude. Parents or choir directors have an important role in this. It's really not helpful to display disappointment at the loss of the treble voice; nothing can be done about it, so don't make the boy feel bad about it.

Puberphonia

This is a very unusual condition in which the boy is reluctant to accept the changes to his voice. He will continue to speak in a high pitch, despite the fact that this will have shifted into falsetto. He may refuse to try out any lower pitches in speaking or singing. It is generally evident that there is a mismatch between the physical maturity of the boy and his speaking pitch. This is a potentially sensitive area and one best dealt with by experts. It is possible to suggest that the boy's speaking voice is not as full and resonant as it could be and that you advise a referral for speech therapy. Once the boy has been seen by a clinically qualified therapist, the therapist will be in a position to recommend other treatments if necessary. Sometimes it can be resolved with a few weeks of speech therapy, or it may need the help of a professional counsellor. Occasionally this issue goes unresolved and the boy may be in his 20s before it is addressed. It can be linked to an Asperger-related pattern of feeling uncomfortable with change (pp. 185–188).

Christopher

He was a shy and awkward boy, obviously ill at ease with his physicality but intelligent and thoughtful. He was 15 years old. He had a strong voice in the soprano range and his speaking voice was centred around B3, just below middle C. This is perhaps slightly higher than a normal treble of his age, and 15 is getting to the upper end of the 'normal' age for the onset of voice change. There was a mismatch though; he was tall and physically mature (facial hair, spots etc.). I knew I could get him to find his lower octave with some vocal play. He was very uncomfortable with what I was trying to do. I tried the usual buzzing and humming; I tried grunting, calling, roaring. He wouldn't go along with any of it, he thought it was all rather silly. In the end I got him coughing, pretending that it was a breathing exercise to loosen the abdomen. Lo and behold, he coughed in his tenor range and I had a way in. We did it again and listened to the sound. I was then able to suggest that there could be more to his voice than he was using at the moment. I didn't criticise his voice use, I didn't suggest that he was doing anything wrong. I merely opened the door to a possibility in the future. I suggested that if he had some speech therapy, it could help his speaking voice become more comfortable and stronger (I didn't say lower).

He was obviously clinging onto the familiar sound of his child-hood voice. He couldn't cope with his adult body and all that it brought with it. However, this was all so subconscious that he accepted my line about comfort and projection in his speaking voice. I also knew that once he had been seen by a speech thera-pist, then he was in the system and clinical referrals for counselling or therapy would follow if necessary. I wrote a quick note to his parents, suggesting that speech therapy might help him (not men-tioning anything more specific).

This happened in a summer school singing lesson and I had no contact with him or his family after this. Then, six months later, I saw him singing again in a concert – as a tenor! He could do it: he was singing tenor and he was proud of himself. He'd been to a speech therapist and was actually grateful for the reason to change. He's still a bit of an odd character, he still can't let anyone near to him physically. However, his voice is healthy and his singing is one of the best things going on in his life. It will help him to deal with all the rest.

If a boy believes that by speaking in falsetto he will 'preserve' his fal-setto voice in order to sing counter-tenor, he is much mistaken. If any individual has been speaking exclusively in falsetto, the muscles of the larynx will be under considerable strain and it may take some time to restore balanced usage. The same can be said for young men who try to sound more 'baritonal' by pushing their speaking voice down, depressing the larynx and lowering the pitch. This can cause considerable strain to the voice in the longer term.

Repertoire for teenage boys

Finding the right repertoire at this stage is a huge challenge. Some boys reduce to a pitch range of about a sixth – there are not many songs you can sing that have this range. Most boys will have about an octave of usable range. However, this limited range will be dropping, and the usable octave in October will not be the same one in December. Singing teach-ers used to rely either on an accompanist who could transpose easily or on writing out the accompaniments by hand. Now we have more possibilities: electric keyboards can play at different pitches, and many published songs are available to download in the key of your choice.

The voice at this stage will have not only limitations of range of movement but also limited ease of movement. The boy will have a smaller difference between quiet and loud singing, he will not find it so easy to change pitch quickly and he will only manage to sustain shorter phrases. What he can do, however, is put enormous amounts of energy and passion into his singing if he's inspired to do so. With this in mind, adolescent boys need to be guided carefully into the right repertoire. Understandably they like to exploit their new manly tones by shouting their way through bombastic songs or arias. However, high-impact vocalising is not to be recommended.

As the boy is growing so rapidly, there will be postural issues to deal with. Many boys develop a habit of pulling the head forward, especially if they are trying to reach high notes. There is a way of using the pharyngeal constrictor muscles (part of the swallowing mechanism) to move and squeeze the thyroid cartilage from above. This can give a semitone or two at the top of the range. It will, however, often result in a pull on the cervical spine (neck), if the deep neck flexors (postural muscles) are not opposing this pull. The net result of this is a throaty sound and a forward head position. These habits may then be carried on through his adult singing. Habits often remain even when the reason for them has gone; the boy may either move to singing baritone, or he may develop an easier high range. Despite these changes, with these habits remaining, he will continue to sing with a high larynx and a squeezed pharynx.

The technical advice for adolescent boys is the same as that for all ages of voice development: not too much high, loud, fast or long. With changing voices these guidelines are even more crucial.

Historical background to singing during adolescent voice change

The question of what is best practice for boys' singing voices during voice change is an ongoing debate. The current advice to boys during voice change tends to be to sing in the lowest comfortable pitch range while the voice is settling into its new range. It is possible, however, that the boy, especially a trained chorister, can sing comfortably with a high tessitura, at least for some of the time, during the early stages of voice change. There were two main schools of thought about this in the USA from the 1950s to the 1970s. The first, or 'limited range' school, believed that boys' voices change predictably, lowering by stages according to an expected form. Irvin Cooper [45] was the originator of this theory (the '**Cambiata**' concept); this approach has been continued by Don Collins (founder of Cambiata Press) and John Cooksey (the 'Eclectic' theory). Cooksey (1992) expanded upon Cooper's work, identifying five stages for the male pubertal voice during change. These are illustrated earlier in this chapter.

The second, or 'extended range' school, believed that boys' voices can change slowly or quickly and may not be limited to a mid-voice comfort range of an octave or less during puberty. Frederick Swanson [46] was the originator of this school, current supporters include Henry Leck [47] and Kenneth Phillips [48].

The key here is that these two schools of thought may not be mutually exclusive – they may both be right. The main difference between the two is that the extended range school advocates the use of falsetto as part of the boy's regular singing, whereas the Cambiata approach is to remain within the lowest comfortable range. The use of occasional falsetto as suggested by the extended range school is not to be confused with the exclusive use of falsetto that will happen if the boy continues to sing as a soprano during puberty. The Cooksey system of five stages may be a useful guide for less experienced teachers and singers. It is relatively simple to grasp, and it is unlikely to be misinterpreted. The 'extended range' school may be more applicable to experienced boy singers, who may have a larger accessible pitch range.

The management of the boy's voice during adolescence is also interesting when cultural and historical perspectives are considered. There are a number of early recordings from the 1930s and 1940s of boy singers using their upper (soprano) pitch range with a high level of vocal artistry and skill. Many of these boys were either in the middle of or almost at the end of puberty. There are one or two rare recordings of spoken interviews with them, in which it is obvious that they are speaking with a lower pitch than an unchanged treble. Many of these young male singers have a sound that is not dissimilar to a mature female voice. There is more power, flexibility and control than in an unchanged male voice and yet a lightness which is not present in an adult male alto singer. We know that it is possible that some boys are able to retain their soprano voices whilst their larynx is growing in power and stamina, especially if these early phases happen relatively fast. The boys on these recordings were reported to have stopped singing when their voices 'broke' (often at the age of 17 or

18). This was often described as a catastrophic overnight event or even as having occurred in a disastrous performance. As this event would have occurred some time after they had undergone adolescent voice change (probably at the age of 14 or 15), it is only possible to guess at what may have precipitated this 'breaking' and what was actually happening physically. This sudden change appears impossible from an anatomical perspective; no part of the body can grow by 65% overnight. What is most likely is that the speaking voice was descending normally but the singing voice was maintained in the high pitch until the whole system suddenly and alarmingly gave way. The muscles of the larynx would have been gradually adapting to maintain the high pitches while they were growing thicker and longer. This would initially give them power and flexibility; but would not be able to last beyond a certain point. It is conceivable that the reported 'breaking' was a sudden inability of the laryngeal structures to sustain this thin-fold phonation, as the larynx became less pliable in early adulthood. This sudden collapse of the singing voice would explain the reported phenomenon of overnight voice change.

No part of the body can grow by 65% overnight.

Currently, maintaining the practice of singing in the soprano range after the onset of voice change is not generally popular amongst boys. They normally want to be seen to be maturing alongside their peers. Late developers generally feel as isolated as the few early developers.

Counter-tenors or male altos

If a boy wishes to sing alto with his adult voice, this is another matter. For some men, this is their most comfortable and flexible vocal range. A good male alto can produce an exquisite sound with enormous expressive ability and he will be able to explore plenty of suitable repertoire. For the sake of allowing the voice, both speaking and singing, to develop with its full potential, I would recommend that the boy allows his baritone range to develop whilst in the middle of voice change, using this for the majority of his singing. It is useful to keep the falsetto sound in exercises during singing lessons, as this encourages flexibility, aids the transition to using the upper pitch range, and can give another colour for specific and occasional use. If it becomes obvious that the boy is eventually more adept using his falsetto range, he can then move to singing in a new upper range. This will have been developed from the basis of baritone singing: shorter, more relaxed vocal folds, better vocal fold closure and air-flow management, and released laryngeal suspensory muscles. This will be a healthier set-up than one that maintains the habits of his treble singing within an adult larynx.

4.6 Allocation of choral parts to voices that are changing

A problem faced by choral directors everywhere is how to allocate traditional soprano, alto, tenor and bass (SATB) parts to individual singers in order to create a balanced choral sound using the singers available. Because of the usual distribution curve of variation within a species, there will be more baritones and second sopranos than anything else. How do we create enough tenors and altos from a group of young singers? Any sort of shoehorning of people into less appropriate voice parts needs to be looked at carefully, so that we balance the needs of the choir with the needs of the individual.

First, it helps to briefly revisit the way the larynx works, in order to find out what happens when we ask it to go outside its normal comfort zone. The larynx has opposing sets of muscles (like nearly all muscle groups in the body) that work against each other in order to raise and lower the pitch. In every voice, there will be a range of pitches within which the laryngeal muscles are most comfortable, where they can operate for the longest time without tiring. An easy way to locate this is to listen to the speaking voice of a singer, as described earlier in this chapter. Once you have the average speaking pitch, you can be fairly sure that the lowest comfortable singing note will be about a third below this. So – from this we can deduce that the larynx is at its happiest near to the bottom of its pitch range. This doesn't mean that it's wrong to try to extend the pitch range from time to time. That's why we learn vocal technique, in order to do this comfortably, safely and with exciting results.

The next job is to work out what is the most comfortable singing range of the individual. Young voices, pre-puberty, will be soprano or alto; again, second sopranos are most common. Deciding on which part is best is mostly to do with overall comfort: look out for pushing or straining either at the top or at the bottom, or listen to where the voice is happiest to project the sound without over-working and you will have a good idea of voice type.

Girls: soprano or alto?

As girls mature through their teens, their voices become richer and some-times lower (occasionally higher). Often they stay on a particular voice part either out of habit, or because they are musically reliable within this part. Regular re-evaluation is very important here. So why do we often ask girls to sing alto when they are normally sopranos? This can be unpopular with the girls involved and so there has to be a very powerful argument in order to justify it. The basic answer is that, without this, there would be a choir with very limited options. There simply wouldn't be enough natural altos to balance the choir parts.

So what happens to the voice when we ask sopranos to sing lower? We know already that the muscles of the larynx are happiest operating in the lower pitches. The singer may not be able to project the sound efficiently, the sound quality may be reduced or compromised, but most importantly – there is no harm done. This means no harm in the short term – voice loss or tiring, and no harm in the longer term – maturation into adult singing. For many girls of this age, some practice using the lower register (speech quality) in a balanced way that allows integration with the mid-dle and upper registers is essential in order to enable the richness of the middle range to develop. For others it may not be ideal, but it's certainly the best compromise all round. For all girls, the challenge of singing (and reading) a part that is not the tune will enhance their musical develop-ment.

Boys: tenor or bass?

Boys' voices are, however, more complicated. The changes during adolescence are much more radical and need to be more carefully monitored and accommodated. This is explained in more detail earlier in this chapter (see the section '**Should a boy continue to sing with his high pitch range?**'). From this we can see that, if the boy continues to sing soprano all the time during voice change, at some point the whole system will collapse. We have seen that it is a good idea for adolescent boys to use falsetto occasionally. What is crucial is that the main body of the singing with a rapidly growing and vulnerable voice is within the fundamental comfort zone – at the lower end of the pitch range. This means that as a general guide, boys should sing in the lowest choral part they can manage. It means that the tenors in a teenage choir will be made up of boys on their way down (stage III) and also settling tenors without top notes yet. Compromise is never easy but nearly always necessary when asking individuals to form a cohesive group.

4.7 The role of parents in singing lessons for adolescents

During the pre-teen years, direct parental involvement is a real advantage for all involved. After a while, however, children need to feel that their singing lessons are their own world and that they are responsible for their own practice. There comes a time when parents have to be asked, politely, to wait outside the room rather than inside. They will understand. If you are making an audio recording of the lesson (p. 127), then this recording is automatically given to the parents anyway, as well as to the pupil. Giving the recording to both parent and pupil is advisable until the pupil leaves school. It means that parents can remain involved as observers and encouragers, but they don't need to try to have too much of a teaching-style input between lessons. It's a tricky one to balance sometimes, but it's best to sort it out before it becomes problematic. At this point children should be wanting to learn, and this should include learning to manage their own time and practice. They can take a while to achieve this (often only getting there in their mid-20s!) but it's a good lesson in itself.

After a while the child needs to think that
the singing lessons are their own world.

Chapter 4 Summary

- Musical tastes developed in adolescence shape individuals' identity and their choice of social groups.
- Adolescents engage with music in some form for an average of 2.5 hours a day.
- The onset of puberty may be slightly earlier than it was 50 years ago. There is no conclusive evidence to show why this may be so.

Adolescent girls:

- The larynx grows by about 34%.
- Growth patterns can result in temporary breathiness or roughness in the voice.
- The onset of the menstrual cycle can also result in periodic roughness in the voice.
- Singing high notes is an unusual sensation, encouragement, exploration and positive role models will help a girl to use this part of her range.

Adolescent boys:

- The larynx grows by about 65%.
- This extreme growth will have had an evolutionary advantage.
- Growth patterns are in five noticeable stages relating to both overall physical growth and the growth of the larynx.
- The speaking pitch is the most reliable indicator of the stage of voice change.
- The high pitch range may continue to be easily accessible after the speaking pitch has lowered. It is advisable to use this part of the voice only occasionally during voice change.
- The comfortable pitch range may reduce considerably, careful choice of repertoire is needed.
- Most boys are happy to accept voice change and enjoy using their new voice.
- Instances where boys are reluctant to acknowledge voice change need to be dealt with sensitively.

Teaching singing technique:

- The same limitations to pitch, loudness and stamina will apply to both teenage girls and boys.
- Boys may have a significantly reduced pitch range (to less than an octave).
- Both boys and girls may adopt compensatory habits to cope with vocal difficulties if they are not given helpful guidance. These habits can remain into their adult singing if they are not addressed.

Changes to the approach to boys' singing over the last 100 years:

- Boys used to be kept singing in the soprano range until their voices were unable to sustain the strain. This resulted not only in a catastrophic collapse (breaking) but also jeopardised their future singing for some time.
- The advice now is to sing in the lowest comfortable range and to use falsetto singing only occasionally.
- If young men feel more comfortable singing in the alto range, this is best developed *after* a year or two of using the baritone range.

Allocation of choral parts:

- It is often necessary to ask singers to join a part less suited to their vocal range.
- It is not intrinsically harmful to a soprano's voice if she is asked to sing alto.
- It is rare to find a teenage boy with a developed tenor range, most tenors of this age will be Stage III boys with a lowering range, or proto-tenors using falsetto for high notes.

The presence of parents in singing lessons may not be helpful for this age group.

Interlude D

Operatic repertoire for ages 18 to 21

Once young singers are at university, there may be opportunities to perform in operas. A number of universities have active operatic societies, generally run by the students themselves. This brings many exciting challenges as well as potential risks for the young singer. The general advice from the teacher has always been that 'big' repertoire is not appropriate; this includes most nineteenth-century operas. Why do these teachers want to spoil the fun of the students?

Looking back over our criteria for repertoire considerations, we know that the young larynx is less capable of vocalisations that are disproportionately long, agile, loud, high or rich in timbre. This limitation lessens as the singer gets older: it is also variable between individuals. Considering now the undergraduate singer, and this includes the younger undergraduates studying at conservatoires, many singers of this age have an impressive vocal technique. They may be able to negotiate the notes and phrases from a variety of operatic roles; they have a mature-sounding vocal timbre, musical intelligence, performing skills and huge amounts of energy. So why should they be limited at all? If they can sing the repertoire, why not learn it and perform it?

In order to investigate this, we need to look firstly at the repertoire in question. The opera houses of Mozart and Handel's day would have seated an audience of between 600 and 1500. The orchestra was relatively small and the orchestration was generally in the interests of the singer, not too heavy during solo passages. During the nineteenth century, opera houses were built to take larger audiences; seating between 1500 and 3000. Professional singers had to develop a vocal technique to match the growing power of the romantic orchestra.

The main problem is not with any individual moments within a role, it is with the vocal stamina needed to sustain an entire role through rehearsal and performance. A rehearsal schedule is never ideal even for professional singers. For students, it is likely to be worse. They have many other simultaneous pressures on their time related to academic work and social activities. Student performances are more likely to be on consecutive nights, in order to optimise use of the performance venue. Student orchestral players may not be as experienced in accompanying soloists as a professional orchestra, and may over-play. All of these factors are set to increase the vocal impact.

High-impact singing for the vocal folds is related to the strength of collision (loudness) and the number of collisions (pitch). When the voice is singing extended music that is loud or high, the vocal folds will become red and inflamed and the voice will tire. This means that the speaking voice may be slightly husky, the upper pitches will not have such a clear onset and quiet singing is less easy. All voice users need vocal recovery time. The soft tissues of the larynx are very quick at repairing as soon as the high-impact voicing stops, but adequate recovery time is crucial. Recovery is, at best, keeping silent: sleep is the best healer of all. When this is not possible, recovery can be helped if the singer makes an effort to limit the voice use. As well as having enough extended time off from rehearsing and performing, it is worth remembering that the more frequent the breaks, the better. An hour's rehearsal with a five-minute break after every ten minutes of singing is better than one with a ten-minute break after every twenty minutes of singing.

If adequate recovery time is not built in, the larynx will have to find other ways of getting the vocal folds to come together. This may include laryngeal constriction (p. 94) or use of the suspensory muscles to re-align the whole system. These habits can then remain beyond the vocal fold recovery. Then longer-term voice problems begin to become an issue, and all from trying to do too much with the voice. These problems are not just from laryngeal fatigue; the overall body will tire. Although the muscles of the torso are stronger and more resilient than the muscles of the larynx, they still work less efficiently when they are tired. If the 'scaffolding' of the voice is not working well (p. 81), the larynx is less able to make subtle adjustments, the smaller muscles of the larynx will then have to make up for the inefficiency of the larger muscles of the torso and the larynx tires much more quickly than it needs to.

How does this relate to the repertoire we are talking about here? This is where the teacher needs to be really familiar with entire roles and not just isolated arias. In fact, there is nothing that can really substitute for actual experience here. If the teacher has performed the role in question, or a similar one, they will be fully aware of the stamina issues. Roles which may be unsuitable are those which demand the singer to use vocalisations that are long: for this, consider the actual number of minutes the singer sings during the opera, as well as the length of individual phrases or set pieces within the opera. Also the roles may be too loud: consider how full the orchestration is, how large the vocal ensembles are, as well as the dynamic writing for the character. Roles which lie consistently high, or which have extended high-lying passages may be too challenging and anything requiring a heavier timbre will cause problems both short and long-term for the young singer.

There may be individual arias that are fine to sing in isolation. It is great to use these for study, and as a way to introduce the singer to the repertoire. However, if the singer uses an operatic aria in an audition, it tends to suggest that she could perform the whole role. The choice of audition aria needs to reflect the current capabilities of the singer.

Chapter 5

How the voice works

5.1 Introduction

In order to give the right guidance to young singers, it can be helpful to have some idea of the workings of the voice. Getting familiar with vocal anatomy can be daunting at first. There seems to be a confusing and endless list of names of all the muscles and cartilages and which ones do what. Then there are the acoustic formants and resonance, the role of the tongue, the jaw and the soft palate. Don't panic! Remember that it will take many repetitions of the information until it begins to make any sort of sense. Also, remember that no one knows everything about how voices work: there are still unexplained mysteries and there are still disagreements between the experts. This chapter will just give a broad outline of the physical nature of the voice and how this applies to singing technique.

Think of it like a car maintenance manual; if you are driving a car, you need to know how to drive and where to put in the fuel. As a singer, this is the equivalent of having a good idea of how to get around your own voice in order to sing the repertoire you choose. A professional singer will need to know a bit more, in the same way as a professional driver of emergency or rally vehicles will. The singing teacher is more like the garage mechanic: he or she needs a working knowledge of the voice that can be applied to more than one voice type. Only when we know what is actually happening can we know what the right course of action may be.

5.2 Posture and breathing

These two areas are too interdependent to be considered as separate entities. Effective breathing can't happen without good posture. Good posture requires balance with alignment. Essentially, the heavy parts of the body need to be lined up over each other, so that the centre of gravity passes through the midline. If you look at the person from the side, could you draw an imaginary straight line through the ear, the shoulder, the hip, the knee and the foot? If these are all in balance, releasing any locked knees, then the singer will be using the minimum of muscular effort in order to stay upright. It may feel unnatural or need some effort – gentle and frequent reminders will gradually lead to a change in habit. Remember that good alignment is a *direction* for the body, not a position. Balanced posture, when the singer is familiar with it, will enable a sense of poise: the body is ready for action without any gripping or holding.

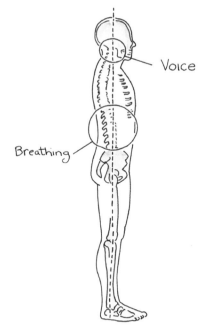

Figure 5.1: Optimum postural alignment enables effective breathing

Head and neck exercise 1

Place your hands around your neck with the fingertips interlinked and gently resting on the cervical spine (neck). The little fingers are under the skull, along the hairline. The thumbs are on the collar-bone – don't allow the thumbs to press on the neck, as this will be uncomfortable. This is a very stable position in which you can monitor the head pulling forward. The arms are out and raised, which can help to stabilise the ribcage also. Try singing whilst maintaining absolute poise in the head and neck, then remove the hands and do the same.

Head and neck exercise 2

Imagine that a trap door is opening at the back of the neck as you sing. This will help to lengthen the back of the neck without allowing it to stiffen or become rigid. The bones in the neck are a series of discs. Imagine that each of them is turning into a marshmallow, they are piled up on top of each other, alternate pink and white. Now realise how soft and squishy they are. Keep them this soft all the time that you are singing.

Head and neck exercise 3

As you are singing, move the head slowly from side to side, only a small amount (so that the nose moves about 2cm from the mid-line each way). As you sing and move your head, you can think the words 'say no to neck tension'.

The old idea of imagining that you are being suspended by a piece of string from the crown of the head is fine if you have good proprioceptive awareness. This is an accurate sense of where your body is in space so, for example, you can tell if one shoulder is lower than the other, or if your hands are behind or in front of your midline. Dancers are very good at this; other children can be surprisingly unaware. Children can be encouraged to lengthen but also to let go, so that their arms and shoulders are hanging loosely. Some will need to soften their alignment, others will need to energise it. Knees will often be gripped, in which case they need to be softened without being bent. Try lengthening the lower back by imagining the tail-bone is falling towards the floor, without actually tucking it under, this allows the lower abdominal muscles to engage – now you are ready to use these for some effective breathing.

Breathing exercise 1

With your thumbs on your navel and your hands resting on the belly, try letting the air out with a long hissing sound and, as you do so, feel your belly moving in towards your back, as if you are trying to get into some pants/trousers which are a size too small. When you have no more air left inside you, release all the tension in your belly muscles (under your hands) and feel it spring outwards as the air drops into your lungs. Careful that as you release, you just let go of the belly muscles and that you don't collapse the ribs as well. The release is the most important part; the harder you work at your singing, the less likely you are to remember to release for the in-breath.

Breathing exercise 2

Once you have got used to the muscles of the belly as the main moving part for getting air in and out of your body, you can extend this hissing to rhythmical patterns. These can be on 'ss' or 'ff' or 'sh'. You can then do the same rhythmical buzzing on voiced sounds like 'zz', 'vv' and 'jj'. Make sure that the rhythms are from your tummy, not from your chest or throat. It will work best if your muscles are quite soft and flexible; coordination is more important than strength.

Breathing exercise 3

Now you have got the hiss working well, try beginning the out-breath with a highly energised rapid 'ffft' and continuing with a long 'shshsh' until you are empty. It is more than likely that your subsequent in-breath will then be an automatic recoil of the abdominal muscles.

Both children and adults will often raise the upper ribs and even the shoulders in an attempt to take in a large amount of air. This gives the sensation of working hard but is generally considered to be not good for singing. The rib lift will create tension in the neck and shoulders. Any over-working in the upper body will probably mean that the singer pulls the belly in during inspiration and collapses the ribs on expiration. You must have heard someone asking you to 'breathe in' when they wanted your waist to go thin – what they are in fact asking for is a rib-lift which will achieve this effect. The singer needs to learn to leave the upper ribs loose and still and to concentrate the movement into the lower part of the abdomen. It is also important to keep the mid-abdomen soft during breathing in and breathing out. Although the muscles here may be involved, they do not need to be actively used. The movement is not in the whole of the wall of the abdomen, it is only in the lower part. Managing breath efficiently for singing is generally a learned skill: it's unlikely to happen automatically without guidance.

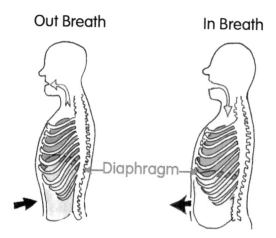

Figure 5.2: *Movement of the lungs and diaphragm for the in-breath and out-breath.*

Once breathing low into the belly has become a habit, the next move is to think about the relationship between breathing and posture. There is a 'zipping up' sensation of movement from the lowest point of the abdomen, up towards the belly button. This 'zipping up' movement extends for the duration of the out-breath. The feeling can be linked with a sensation of lengthening through the spine and widening through the back. This will be linking breathing and posture in a positive way (see automatisms, p. 37).

It may be worth noting that dancers are trained to hold their abdominal muscles while they are dancing. This is in order to maintain stability in the core support and is essential in order to prevent back injuries. A singing pupil who is also a dancer will have to make adjustments and rethink his habitual body use. Of course there will be conflicts when performers are required to sing and dance at the same time. This will require some individual compromise as well as sympathetic choreography.

Another way to check that the breathing action is using the right muscles is to feel the waist. Ask the singer to put her hands onto her waist (find the softest bit between ribs and hips). The hands will go into their body as she breathes in, and then will be pushed out by the muscle as she sings. Moving the attention to the waist can be helpful in distributing and balancing the movement. Sometimes a young singer will be keen to show how well he is learning the flexible abdominal movement, this can result in 'belly dancing to please the teacher' rather than effective and economical breathing technique.

What is 'support'?

This term is so often misused or misunderstood that many people I know tend to avoid it when teaching. If you ask an inexperienced singer to 'support more', you may find that all they do is hold or grip the middle of their tummy. This is definitely not helpful for any singer, so what do we mean by the term? The definition of the word 'support' is more to do with maintaining stability than with applying specific effort. In terms of voice use, the stability required from support relates to providing appropriate air flow and air pressure. If you think about it, the precise air pressure needed will vary continuously. It will be slightly different for each vowel, change of pitch, variation in loudness, and it will alter depending on where the singer is within the phrase. Such intricate variables are far too complex to adjust on a conscious level. This is something that the body will regulate extremely well on its own, if you allow it the flexibility to do so.

Belly balancing exercise

If any part of the body is exerting too much tension, the best way to detect this and then to eliminate it is to give a little wiggle. First try drawing horizontal circles with the hips, circling them round and round. Then try doing small hip circles whilst hissing and then whilst buzzing. The next step is to keep wiggling the hips round and round but now whilst singing. This shouldn't interfere with the sound at all.

The best approach is to set up a breathing system that will provide a basic level of constant output, which is subtly adjustable throughout. This does sound very complicated, but the essence here is flexibility: gentle movement without too much effort. If this part of the breathing is right, the rest will happen automatically. If the phrase tails off in energy or goes flat, this is often a sign that the breath management is not quite right. The singer needs to set up balanced posture and effective breathing, aiming for economy of movement and effort. For the young singer, support needs to be no more than this, anything effortful is probably overdoing it.

What is the role of the diaphragm?

You may have heard singing teachers and choral directors asking their pupils to 'sing from the diaphragm'. This is not only hard to visualise but also anatomically impossible. The diaphragm is a dome-shaped muscle lying within the ribcage. The lower edges insert into the lower ribs. The upper part of the dome lies high within the ribs: at rest it is level with the nipples. You can see the location of the diaphragm in the picture on p. 85. Because of the deeply internal position of the diaphragm, we can't feel it at all, no matter how hard we probe our midriff. As a vital life-preserving muscular action, it is governed by the autonomic nervous system and has no sensory nerve endings – this means that we have no idea whether it is contracting or relaxing – so we can't see it and we can't feel it.

As the diaphragm contracts it pulls air into the lungs, and it then releases while we breathe out. This is only one of the ways in which we can pull air into our lungs: breathing can be intercostal (ribs), clavicular (upper ribs and shoulders) or diaphragmatic (this will cause a bulge in the abdomen). So yes, we want diaphragmatic breathing for inhaling when we sing. The key point here is that when we sing, we are breathing out; so the diaphragm actually relaxes as we sing.

So – we can't see the diaphragm, we can't feel it and it is relaxing as we sing. All of these facts suggest that any mention of the diaphragm with relation to singing is fairly pointless. This doesn't mean to say that it's not important; we need to ensure that the in-breath is made predominantly with the diaphragm and not with the ribs and shoulders. This will happen automatically if our posture is set up as suggested earlier; making any reference to the diaphragm unnecessary.

For the more experienced singer, there is a link between activity in the diaphragm and some control of air on the out-breath. When the lungs are full of air, there is pressure from the natural elasticity of the lungs to push the air out. If the airflow is not regulated by the breathing muscles, it will come out as a whoosh and then a fizzle: a whole rush of air, followed by a trickle. When singing, especially at the start of a phrase, there is a sense of connection with the breathing-in muscles. The singer thinks about the sensation of breathing in for the first moments of the out-breath. This is a very gentle thought, nothing is held or stiff in the upper torso: it will keep the airflow more constant. It is the equivalent of gently applying the brakes whilst freewheeling downhill.

5.3 The primary sound source: the larynx

Voicing happens in the larynx. You can feel this in the front of your neck as a lump about a third of the way down, the size of a small egg, which vibrates when you speak. The larynx is a very mobile container made of

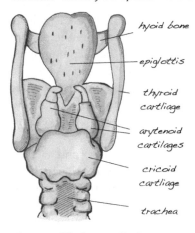

several cartilages (these are a bit softer than bone). Within these are the vocal folds – two tiny strips of membrane about 17mm long in children, 23mm in women and 28mm in men. As the air comes up from the lungs, through the larynx, these vocal folds collide and wobble. Just to give you an idea of how much: if you sing a middle C, these folds are colliding about 260 times a second. The muscles within the larynx move the cartilages around in order to change the length and thickness of the vocal folds. These movements alter the pitch, loudness and some basic voice

Figure 5.3: The Larynx: Back view.

qualities. The larynx itself doesn't have many nerve endings we can feel: the sensation of the vocal folds colliding hundreds of times a second would be far too uncomfortable! However, it is very highly sensitised to foreign objects entering it, and this will trigger a cough immediately. So, we can't feel the surface of the vocal folds themselves and we can't feel the muscles working within the larynx. This makes it tricky to start carrying out conscious changes. Nevertheless, looking at this from another angle, we know that we are capable of hundreds of emotive noises with very subtle variations. Learning to sing is really channelling these noises by giving them pitch and rhythm, and then assigning words to them.

The larynx is a collection of cartilages and bone suspended by muscles and ligaments at the top of the windpipe. The lower cartilage (cricoid) is a complete ring, on the upper back edge of this are two small and very mobile cartilages (arytenoids). Hinged onto the cricoid is the largest of the cartilages (thyroid), which forms an incomplete ring (with the gap at the back). The thyroid cartilage can be seen and felt (Adam's Apple). At the top of the larynx is the hyoid bone, which is also attached to the base of the tongue. There are several groups of muscles that connect these cartilages and move their positions relative to each other and as a whole unit within the throat. Suspended from them on the inside are the vocal

In the figure, the following labels are shown: *hyoid bone*, *epiglottis*, *thyroid cartilage*, *arytenoid cartilages*, *cricoid cartilage*, *trachea*.

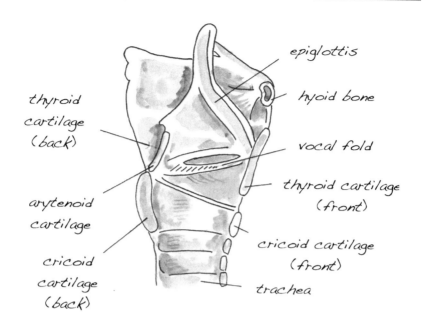

Figure 5.4: The structure of the larynx.

folds: two strips of tissue (comprising muscle, ligament and mucosa) that can be pushed or pulled together to close the gap at the top of the wind-pipe.

One of the main problems we have as singers is that the vocal mechanism, primarily the larynx and the throat, are not designed solely for singing and speech. The primary function of the larynx is as a valve. If the larynx closes tight, the top of the windpipe is sealed and particles of food cannot enter the lungs when we swallow. This closing action is crucial for our survival; as such it is often a default tendency of the whole system. If there is an unfamiliar sensation, the larynx will instinctively get ready to close shut. The secondary function of the larynx is to close in order for us to lift or push. If the hole at the top of the windpipe is left open, we can't use the muscles of the torso to help with pushing or lifting, as the effort ends up merely pushing air out of the lungs. When we use strong physical actions we need to build up pneumatic pressure within the torso with a closed larynx.

Attached to the inside front edge of the thyroid cartilage is a cartilage flap (epiglottis), like a trap-door, which also assists in closing the windpipe when we swallow. The larynx lifts, squeezes and tips forwards so that the epiglottis is pushed over the top of it. This valving action is what the larynx does best. The fortunate by-product of this structure is that if the vocal folds are brought together more gently as we are breathing out, they vibrate to make a sound. The basic sound made by the larynx alone is a buzzing noise; this is then amplified and filtered by the vocal tract.

The vocal folds

The **frequency** of vocal fold collisions determines the pitch of the sound. Middle C has a frequency of about 260Hz; a violin string playing the same pitch will be vibrating the same number of times per second. The pitch (frequency) of this sound can be raised by elongating the vocal folds, or by increasing the subglottic pressure. The muscles responsible for lengthening are principally the **cricothyroid** muscles. The muscles responsible for shortening (lowering the pitch) are the **thyroarytenoid** muscles.

Loudness is related to the degree of impact, determined by the contact area of the vocal folds and the speed of closure (related to the distance travelled by the vocal fold during each vibratory cycle). Try clapping your hands quietly and then loudly; for louder clapping you will be moving your hands more, clapping them together harder and using the whole surface of the palm. Loudness in the voice (amplitude) can be raised by increasing the force of collision of the vocal folds, or by increasing the subglottic pressure.

The colour (timbre) can be altered by adjusting the thickness of the vibrating edges (to over-simplify: thick = chest register, thin = head register, thin and stiff = falsetto) and by adjusting the height of the larynx within the throat. The height of the larynx will determine the length of the vocal tract (from the vocal folds to the lips). Longer tubes make warmer sounds.

The outer layer of vocal fold tissue is known as the mucosal layer. When the vocal folds come together, they close with a rolling action from the bottom to the top of the vocal fold. This sets up a wave around the edge of each vocal fold (mucosal wave), which in turn generates turbulence in the sound wave, enhancing upper partials in the frequency spectrum and defining the basic vocal timbre. The second layer within the mucosal layer on the tip of the vocal fold is a jelly-like sac called Reinke's space. This is partly what enables the outer layer of the vocal fold to have its characteristic wobble, or mucosal wave.

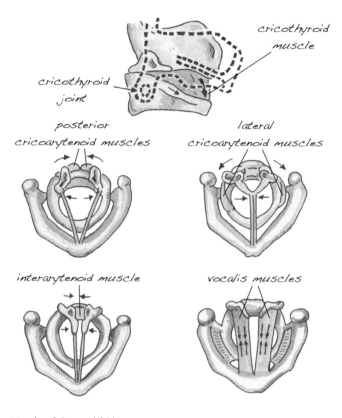

Figure 5.5: Muscles of the vocal folds.

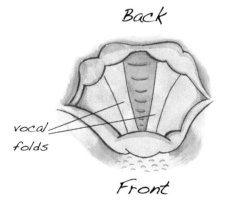

Figure 5.6: A view of the vocal folds from above.

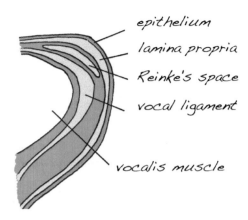

Figure 5.7: Vocal fold layers.

Chest and head registers

Chest register (speaking quality) is made by vibrating thick vocal folds. As there is a greater area of contact, the possibility of strain is reduced as long as the pitch is at the lower end of the range. Remember that our habitual speaking pitch is normally about three or four semitones higher than our lowest comfortable singing note. **Head register** is made by thinning as well as elongating the vocal folds and is normally used at a higher pitch. Both chest and head registers (or speech quality and thin-fold) are known as **modal** voice. The link between them is that the vocal folds are colliding with the same vibratory pattern moving through them.

Falsetto

True falsetto is different from thin-fold vibration; male altos use both qualities. True falsetto is caused when the **vocalis** muscle releases and goes flaccid; the **arytenoid** cartilages are swung back and up, thinning and stiffening the vocal folds. The tension within the vocal fold is provided primarily by the vocal ligament, rather than by the muscle of the vocal fold body. The vocal ligament is part of the inner layer of the vocal fold mucosa. It runs the full length of the vocal fold, from the thyroid cartilage at the front, to the vocal process of the arytenoid cartilage at the back. It is not well developed in the young larynx, although some layering can be seen in children from the age of 5 or 6, the vocal ligament does not become significantly definable until adolescence.

Falsetto sound is caused by the vibration of the outer mucosal layer, the vocal folds themselves do not have the same vibratory pattern as they do in modal singing. It cannot be made with increased air pressure and so has little dynamic range. The resulting sound can be hooty and breathy: it is used by many inexperienced singers in the upper part of their range. Because this sound relies on the tensile strength of the vocal ligament, it is not generally used by younger children as their vocal ligament is not so well-developed.

Vibrato

The fluctuations in pitch and intensity that are heard in vibrato can be voluntary or involuntary. The voluntary kind I will call **wobble**, the involuntary kind I will call **intrinsic vibrato**. They both have a place in vocal music; intrinsic vibrato tends to feature throughout the sound in trained adult classical singing. There is a natural phenomenon caused by the time it takes to transmit a signal along the nerve, which can be seen in all muscles of the body as a tremble. If the muscle in question is activated to a particular extent, the signal to contract is engaged and disengaged at a frequency of about six per second. This can either be due to muscle fatigue, or it can be as a result of antagonistic muscle pairs working against each other in a specific manner. In singing the nerve tremor corresponds to the natural frequency of oscillation of the larynx. If the singer has the optimum balance of muscle use within the larynx these fluctuations are audible. The effect is one of simultaneous fluctuations of pitch, loudness and timbre as well as of reducing vocal fatigue. As an intrinsic vibrato (one which is not a conscious wobble) is generally the result of optimum muscle balance: it tends to occur in trained voices, whereas a wobble can be produced by any singer. Intrinsic vibrato cannot easily be 'switched off' if a trained classical singer is in mid-flow. Wobble can be made by shaking the tongue root against the top of the larynx, or by shaking the larynx itself.

Larynx-loosening wobble exercise

Sing a sustained note to 'ah'. Stand on one leg, sing the note and half-way through it shake your foot. The shaking foot wobbles the body and this wobbles the larynx. This exercise can be used as a starter for learning to trill.

Intrinsic vibrato is uncommon in children; it tends to emerge during puberty. This could be due to the maturation of the vocal ligament. This structure within the vocal folds gives some tensile strength to the vibrating folds and reduces the work within the thryoarytenoid muscle. This reduction in the muscle contraction could be enough to enable the subtle balance of muscle action that is needed for vibrato to occur. Although children may not sing with an intrinsic vibrato, as I describe it, they may choose to use a wobble to flavour a note: this is a matter of taste and style.

Creak

This sound is like a creaky door. If you go right to the bottom of the pitch range in a loose, relaxed way, the voice will naturally go into creak. When low in pitch and relaxed (deconstructed), it is safe and healthy. If it is used as a stylistic choice for a type of onset, it need not cause any problems (this would be in Contemporary Commercial Music (CCM), not classical styles). If it is observed in everyday speech to any great extent, often at the ends of phrases, it can be a sign of a tired or unhealthy voice.

Constriction

One important area of potentially harmful tension can be larynx constriction. This can be heard as harshness in the sound, eventually leading to cracking. Remember how good the larynx is at closing, it will go towards this action if there is any unfamiliarity or discomfort, or pressure from the breath. Constriction is part of the way to a swallowing reflex, leading to the false vocal folds being pressed in and down onto the true vocal folds. This can result in a chaotic vocal fold vibration, audible as harshness.

If the in-breath is noisy, this can show that there is some constriction in the larynx. The tightness of the larynx is enough to cause turbulence in the incoming air that can be heard. Noisy inhalation can also be a sign of bronchial constriction, either from bronchitis or asthma. If you hear a noisy in-breath, do ask the child if he is asthmatic; if he is, you may not be hearing laryngeal constriction (see asthma, Chapter 8). Laryngeal constriction is used in pop distortion singing. If the underlying vocal technique is good and the sound is clear, then distortion can be applied – this is heard as a sort of growl. However, in the same way as belting (p. 100) – it's for special effect only, not for an entire song. If in doubt, don't do it.

De-constriction exercise 1

Take a silent breath in. Sing gentle exercises using the buzzing noises described in the breathing section, or sing on a lip trill (singing through vibrating lips, like a child imitating a motorbike) or a rolled 'r'. As you do so, focus on a general physical release around the head and neck and especially a sense of internal smiling (within the throat, not the face) or silent giggling.

De-constriction exercise 2

Try making a sound with a breathy, low-pitched onset. It is very difficult to do this with a constricted larynx. Now try this with 'puffy cheeks' – this is a way of singing with the mouth nearly closed, the sound coming out between the lips but with the cheeks puffing out. Sing a sliding descending perfect fifth to the bottom, or near-bottom of your range with this sound. Let the bottom note feel really loose. Then try this again and slide back up the fifth, then down again to an open 'ah'. This should feel very loose and open (de-constricted).

De-constriction detector 3: The Siren

You should ideally be able to slide through their entire vocal range on a 'ng' sound, **quietly** (comfortably quiet), **clearly** (no breathiness or cracking) and **smoothly** (no bumps or gaps in the slide). This will demonstrate balanced, efficient and healthy sound production in the larynx. Careful that the 'ng' is the sound at the end of the word 'sing', not 'sung'; the tongue will be further back for the 'sung'. It sometimes helps to make a slow and gentle chewing action while doing this exercise, as this can help to release tongue root tension at the same time. If you are sirening in the upper part of your pitch range, let the sound feel small and possibly a bit squeaky. If you try and make it beautiful or projected, you may push it which will defeat the object of the exercise.

Onset

The activity of the vocal folds is also responsible for the **onset** of the sound. There are four different onsets:

- A **glottal onset** is created by the vocal folds coming together before the air passes through; as it bursts through the closed vocal folds an audible 'click' can be heard. This onset can be used as emphasis for words beginning with a vowel: we use it all the time in our everyday speech. Think of impending disaster and say 'uh – oh'. Each of these sounds will have a glottal onset.
- An **aspirate onset** results from the air flow starting before the vocal folds come together, as in words beginning with an 'h' (say 'hey-ho' and you've got it).
- **Simultaneous onset** requires greater coordination between the laryngeal muscles and the airflow; this is the ideal way to sing words beginning on a vowel (unless you choose to do otherwise for stylistic reasons).
- **Creak onset** is a special effect (or a bad habit).

Onset exercise 1

This is to practise the difference between the first three types of onset, it will also help to reduce breathiness. Firstly sing 'hee, hee, hee' as separate sounds on the same note. This is the breathy onset. Then sing an 'ee' or [i] vowel with a glottal click – this is the 'uh, oh' sound we make when facing a problem or disappointment. Now try and make the click as light as you can and sing the repeated 'ee, ee, ee' vowel with a click on each one. Lastly, sing the 'ee' vowel as if you were starting it with an imagined or silent 'h'. The onset will be clean, not breathy and not clicked. This exercise is most effective if done quietly and gently.

Onset exercise 2: Ski Jumps

Once you have managed to begin a sound with the three types of onset, you can use these in exercises. Sing a fairly fast ascending fifth to a vowel (start with 'ee' and then change to other vowels). Pause for a moment at the top and then slide down again. The pause should have a feeling of suspension mid-air, as if you had left the ground for a moment. Try beginning each slide with a gentle glottal onset, and then try a gentle glottal offset as well. This is the same feeling in reverse: the vocal folds come together to stop the sound. When you have this exercise easy, clear and smooth, you can try it with semi-vowels, w and y, to begin the sound. Eventually you can progress to simultaneous onsets and offsets.

Breathiness

This is caused by air escaping through the glottis during vocalising. Some breathiness in the sound is normal for young voices. Taking this into account, it is generally possible to reduce levels of breathiness and often to eliminate it. Although the coordination to bring the vocal folds together cleanly is not as developed in young voices, working on this will assist in smoothing register changes and in the development of a more efficient sound.

Breathiness can be used for effect if the singer wishes to sound intimate or vulnerable but this breathy sound cannot be projected. There are at least three ways to go about reducing breathiness. You can try working with a very gentle glottal onset, or reducing the airflow, or enhancing resonance (resonance pp. 107–8, vowel modification p. 111). Many children will find reducing breathiness hard to address, especially in their higher pitch range or,

Breathy voice ....

for girls, during puberty (p. 60). It is, however, still possible to reduce breathiness at any stage, as you are working on specific muscle groups in order to do this.

Breathiness exercise 1

Use a creak onset at a very low pitch in a quiet, loose, easy way. If you can slow the creak down to individual pops, it is a sign of a balanced larynx and healthy vocal folds. Use this sound for the onset of vowels in speech and singing. Then try the sound without the creak onset and see if the breathiness has reduced.

Breathiness exercise 2

Try three short separated sounds on an open vowel with a very gentle glottal onset. These could be stepwise notes (mi, re, do) or a triad (so, mi, do). Once this can be done clearly and easily, join the three notes together with a glottal onset on the first one. Then try this on different pitches, gradually extending the range upwards.

Pitch range

The pitch range of a singer is determined by the length of the vocal folds and the flexibility of the larynx. The lower range cannot generally be extended, even with training, while the upper range can. As a rule of thumb, one would expect children from ages 3 to 5 to have a comfortable singing range of C4 to C5, ages 6 to 9 from Bflat3 to E5 and ages 10 to 13 from Aflat3 to G5. There is, of course, some variation between individuals; for example, the extended upper range can give up to another octave in some singers.

| 0 - 2 yrs | 4 yrs | 6 yrs | 8 yrs | 11 yrs |

Key: x = speech F$_0$, ● = speech range, o = singing range.

Figure 5.8: Pitch ranges of children in speaking and singing

Register change

The most noticeable **register change** in children is the primary shift from speech quality ('chest voice') to the upper vocal range ('head voice'). Many children find this a problematic shift as they are not used to singing in their upper range. The lower range, or speech quality, is strong and projects well. It is the vocal register we instinctively use for shouting. The upper range can be what we use for calling ('yoo-hoo'). It relies more on the use of resonance to project the sound and may need to be cultivated and encouraged. This register shift generally occurs at about C5 or D5 in children. This is a higher pitch than adult females, which would generally be at G4/A4, although it is lower for trained classical singers (D4) and higher for trained musical theatre singers (C5). The noticeable quality change in children is not as great as the adult shift; the child vocal folds are thinner, making a less obvious transition from thick to thin.

As the voice makes the transition from 'chest' to 'head' voice, the vocal folds will thin out as they lengthen. We know that higher pitches are made with longer vocal folds, so it makes sense that they thin out as they lengthen (like rubber bands). We also know, however, that the transition from thick to thin folds can be made over a large range of pitches. There are many notes within the vocal range that can be sung with either voice quality. It can in theory be done over the entire vocal range, although the sound of thin-fold singing at very low pitches and that of thick-fold singing at very high pitches is hopelessly inefficient and very quiet! So, although thick- or thin-fold singing is related to pitch, this is only part of the story.

The choice of voice quality can, over the mid-range, be purely a stylistic choice. Singing in either register can be healthy voice use. If thick-fold singing is taken to higher pitches, it can then either be transformed into 'belting', or it can merely become a 'shouty' habit, a type of security mechanism that will dissuade the child from using thin-fold singing. In this case the upper vocal range is often weaker and less popular with the singer. Progress can be made with practice and some work on the use of resonance. An extremely effective way to find higher pitches is through vocal play. Whooping, calling, wailing, mewing and crying are all ways of finding clear, projected sound in the upper register. This can then be given pitch, duration and eventually text, turning it into singing.

Belting

This is a style of singing used in musical theatre, and some pop and rock repertoire. There are different types of belting, but in general it is a high-impact sound in the upper vocal range made with thick-fold vibrations, a high percentage of vocal fold closure per cycle and often a high degree of twang (pp. 107–8) in the sound. In very basic terms, it is taking a shout and making it sustainable on a given pitch and with text. In order to do this without harming the larynx, it is essential to regulate the airflow (reduce it to less than one would expect) and to deconstrict the laryngeal muscles. It is also necessary to secure the posture of the head and neck to give the optimum stability for the system. It is important to note that belting is for special occasions only: it is a dramatic effect for the point of climax only – perhaps two or three bars of a song. Any more than this would result in the impact being lost (and the singer getting too tired!).

Is this suitable for young voices? It is going to contribute significantly to vocal loading, and it could be potentially tiring or even abusive for the vocal folds. On the other hand, if you tell children not to sing in a particular way, they are likely to continue doing so, but unsupervised and in private. In my opinion, it is better to teach them how to do it, let them do it in lessons and then try to suggest that it may not be the right thing for public performance just yet! Bear in mind that children have thinner

vocal folds than adults, and the degree of closure won't be as great. They won't get the really big impact that adult voices can get, this means that they can't and shouldn't copy adult sounds. The next thing is to know the possibilities and limitations of the child's voice. Some children have a facility for high belty singing (up to F5), for example, the type used in the show Annie, whereas others can't take their thick-fold voice beyond A4. Using twang can help to reduce the vocal loading of belt; it is also a safe way to achieve a similar voice quality if belting is too difficult or causing problems.

5.4 The vocal tract: the throat, mouth and nose

As a general summary, the vocal tract is very flexible: the singer can alter both its length and also its width at various points. The sound coming directly from the larynx is a sort of buzzing noise. In order to refine this into either intelligible speech or beautiful singing we rely on the shape of the throat and mouth and the position of the jaw, tongue and soft palate. These moving parts will alter vowel sounds and resonant qualities such as brightness or roundness in the tone, for example. If the tongue is raised in the mouth with the lift towards the front, you will create an [i] vowel, flatten the tongue and you have an [ɑ] or raise the back and you have an [u].

The vocal tract is the tube extending from the vocal folds to the lips or nostrils. The length of the vocal tract can be altered by the height of the larynx. As we saw in Chapter 2, the larynx sits higher in children and this part of the system is less flexible as a result. If you purse your lips forward, you lengthen the vocal tract (the resonant tube) resulting in a darker sound; if you widen them in a cheesy grin, you shorten the vocal tract, resulting in a brighter sound (just as the descant and treble recorder have different sound qualities even when playing the same pitch).

The soft palate is a mobile plug, it lifts to seal the space between the mouth and the nose so that when you swallow, your food goes into your stomach, not into your nose. If you raise it when you sing, you get a bigger resonant space for the sound; if you drop it when you sing, you get a nasal sound (useful either for specific characterisation or some French vowels). If the soft palate is slightly lowered, you get a nasal-oral mix which can be used in some musical theatre or country and western styles.

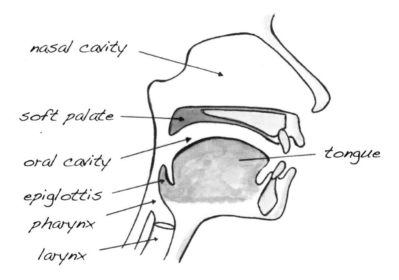

Figure 5.9: The vocal tract.

Swallowing

The pharynx is a muscular sleeve attached to the skull at the top and the larynx at the bottom. Its primary function is to create an action that will enable us to swallow food: passing the food from the mouth into the oesophagus whilst effectively closing the back of the nose and the top of the windpipe.

This swallowing action is achieved by the contraction of the pharyngeal constrictor muscles, the raising and squeezing of the larynx, the raising of the soft palate and the action of the tongue. This is not a good combination of actions for voice use.

Yawning

This is a reflex action designed to open the throat, allowing air to go in easily, in order to raise our oxygen intake if we are tired. The soft palate rises (good for singing) and the back of the tongue pushes the larynx down and back. This movement of the tongue opens the throat to enable more air to enter but also 'fixes' the larynx and restricts mobility. A complete yawning sensation whilst singing is really unhelpful (try speaking and yawning simultaneously) – see **tongue root tension**, p.106.

Yawning is bad?

The shape of the pharynx in singing

The general advice for singers is to use an 'open throat'. This is a rather ambiguous term, as it is the constrictions within the vocal tract that give the sound its resonant qualities. We could not produce any sort of ringing tone, or indeed sing on different vowels, without the right sort of constrictions. What we are aiming for is a vocal tract without unnecessary tension. The wrong sort of constrictions will inhibit the balance of the larynx, tongue and soft palate. In general, if the singer can feel any sort of stretching or squeezing, try to get him to release these. Singing with a balanced vocal system will probably feel as if very little is actually happening.

Sound waves travel in straight lines: if sound is bounced off relatively hard surfaces it will carry further than if the sound is absorbed by softer tissues. Harder surfaces include the raised (stretched) soft palate and the hard palate. Softer surfaces include the nasal cavity.

Groups of harmonics of the note itself are components of pharyngeal tone (p.119). The role of the pharynx as a resonator is to reinforce some of these groups, depending on the vowel or timbre required. There are many factors that alter the shape of the pharynx. The larynx can move up and down (affecting the length of the vocal tract): this is controlled by the relationship between the suspensory muscles, part of the swallowing mechanism, and the strap muscles that lower the larynx. The cartilages can tilt independently of each other to aim the sound waves at different parts of the pharynx. The soft palate can move both up and down and can be raised in a wide arch or a taller, narrower arch.

The base of the tongue can be used to block or direct sound. If the tip of the tongue is forward in the mouth and the middle section of the tongue is raised (the portion between the back teeth) this can help to lift the back of the tongue out of the throat.

The position of the jaw is important in determining the position and flexibility of the tongue and larynx because of the connections between the muscles responsible: any extremes of jaw movement are detrimental. Finally, maintaining a stable position of the head and neck (balanced posture again) is crucial in order to give all of these parts the freedom to function at their optimum.

Tone production is a subjective and stylistically specific matter. There are, however, some issues of vocal tract tension that are counter to maintaining healthy singing in any style.

Jaw tension

Ideally the jaw should be hanging loose, with the actual mouth opening varying according to the vowel, pitch and dynamic being sung. Tension in the jaw can be observed as immobility (gripping) or a forward position. This movement will pull on the back of the throat and the top of the larynx as well as limiting tongue mobility. Choral conductors may ask their singers to open their mouths wide – this is probably because they like to see their singers being involved, not because it necessarily has any positive effect on the sound. Overextension of the jaw can be detrimental to both the sound and to vocal health due to the tensions it creates in the system.

Jaw exercise 1

Placing the fingertips on the jaw hinge just in front of the ears. Move the jaw up and down a little: you will feel small movements under your fingers. Now open your mouth as wide as you can: you will feel the bone move out and forward. It is this movement that is not good for singing. See how much up and down movement you can get without this pull forward.

Encourage the jaw to hang; any gripping in the biting muscles will harden the sound. The jaw itself has very little to do with helping us to sing well. It is primarily for eating and best left for that purpose.

Jaw exercise 2

This exercise uses the thumb between the teeth to immobilise the jaw during singing. Initially try gently biting the tip of the thumb with the thumbnail on the lower front teeth and the thumb knuckle sitting on the chin. It should be possible to sing entire phrases in this position; the singer will have to work hard with the tongue tip to try to articulate the text. Then try rotating the thumb so that it sits on its side between the teeth. This enables the jaw to release into an easier, hanging position and the tongue still has to work hard. Check afterwards to see if there are tooth marks on the thumb – if there are, this shows jaw gripping!

Jaw exercise 3

When you have the jaw able to release and hang, you can keep a check on it by putting the fingers on the cheeks and feeling the space between the teeth, from the outside. It is possible to feel if the back teeth are apart, but only if the biting muscles are soft.

The tongue

The tongue is not flat, it is a ball of muscle. If you put out your tongue, you only see the front third, the rest is still inside the mouth and throat. The movement of the tongue is extremely complex and it is not necessary to know how the individual muscles work. It is important, however, to know that the back of the tongue is connected to the hyoid bone; therefore any pulling back, or back and down, with the tongue will press down on the hyoid bone which in turn will press down on the larynx. This action is often mistaken for one that will 'open the throat' (as in a yawning sensation) whereas it will actually have the opposite effect.

The tendency among singers is either to have a fixed tongue or an inactive tongue. There are no 'correct' positions for the tongue, it needs to remain flexible at all times in order to be free for energised articulation of vowels and consonants.

Tongue tension can be felt by placing the thumb under the chin, behind the jawbone. Any consistent downward pressure on the thumb indicates tongue tension, which will be pressing not only onto your thumb, but also directly onto the top of the larynx. Again, some teachers may ask their singers to sing with a 'yawning' sensation. Although this may help as a pre-singing stretch, if it is employed during singing this is most likely to cause unpleasant degrees of tongue root tension (see also **choral singing** p. 174).

Jaw and tongue root exercise 1

Sing a descending scale (or another familiar exercise) with 'yaya' on each note. First do this while gently biting your thumb (see Jaw exercise) – this will keep your jaw still and make your tongue work harder. Next place your thumb under your chin, feeling the soft part just behind the jawbone and sing the scale again – feel your tongue moving but not pressing down. Keep your jaw loose and not moving forward.

Tongue root exercise 2

Sing a descending scale (or another familiar exercise) with your tongue stuck out of your mouth as far as it will go – this looks very silly, don't worry! Now do this again, but at the start of each note, with your tongue sticking right out, bite onto your tongue to make a 'th' onset. As you release the teeth/tongue for the vowel, allow your tongue to spring back to a place just behind your lower teeth. Do this for each note, it's not easy but it will really get your tongue root stretched and loose.

Singers may pull the tongue back in their mouth in order to enhance their own perception of their voice. Much of our own aural perception of our voice is from the sound conducted through the bones and tissues of the head. Bones are better at conducting low frequencies and so this internal sound tends to appear richer and darker. If the tongue is pulled back, it helps to channel the sound internally towards our own ears. When a singer releases habitual tongue root tension, they often feel that their voice has become smaller or thinner. Everyone knows that a recording of their speaking voice sounds different from their own perception. This is where an external audio recording can help them to appreciate the deception of this sensation.

Projected resonance

This is not just making the sound louder; it is enhancing certain frequencies in the sound in order to create a 'ringing' quality in the sound. This is the main 'carrying' element of the singing and speaking voice: it's a very useful way of making the voice seem louder with little extra effort.

Resonance exercise

Sing any exercise or tune you like with a very nasal 'nyaa' sound on each note. Make sure that you are not constricting the larynx as you do so. Keep the jaw soft and not opened too much. You may feel vibrations in the front of your face or the roof of your mouth. Then repeat this on a 'na' sound, keeping the intensity of the vibrations but with a less nasal sound. You can also do this using a cat's meow, a duck's quack or a witches' cackle, they will all find and enhance the ringing resonance.

Nasality

The **soft palate** can be raised or lowered during singing; a lowered soft palate will result in a nasal sound. It is important to distinguish between this nasal sound and a sensation of vibration across the bridge of the nose. This sensation is caused by vibrations of sound energy against the hard palate and into the skull. These are a result of enhanced resonance created in the vocal tract: the sound is not actually in the nasal cavity, the head or the front of the face. The ringing sound or twang described above can be either nasal or oral. It is generally advisable to sing with a raised soft palate as the sound will be brighter and more resonant. The soft palate may drop if there is tongue root tension. One of the main muscles helping to raise the soft palate is fixed at both ends to the back of the tongue. If the tongue is pulling back and down, the soft palate can't rise. This is sometimes more evident on certain vowels, such as [o].

Soft palate exercise 1

Sing an extended [a] vowel and, halfway through, hold your nose and then let go again. Does the sound quality alter? If so, some of the sound was going into your nose and your [a] vowel is nasal. Do this again and feel when the sound is vibrating only in your mouth. If this is the case, your soft palate is lifted.

Soft palate exercise 2

Sing an exercise with an energetic 'ba' on each note – if the soft palate is dropped, the 'b' consonant will be more of a 'm'. Feel the build-up of air in the mouth just before you release the consonant. This air will only build up if there is a complete seal at the back of the mouth with a lifted soft palate. Try the exercise with 'ngee' on each note, pronouncing the 'g' at the end of the 'ng'. As you do so, feel the back of the mouth spring upwards way from the tongue. Now try this to 'ga, gee' and 'ka, kee' and feel the same lift at the back.

Vowels

These are made almost entirely by the position of the tongue within the mouth. As the tongue creates spaces and constrictions within the vocal tract, the size and shape of the resonant spaces are altered. This enhances or dampens specific upper partials or formants in the acoustic spectrum, giving some shapes 'darker' qualities and some 'brighter' ones. The position of the tongue to create clear vowels will need to be slightly different for each pitch. With some external guidance from the teacher, the singer can learn the sensation of finding the 'middle' of a note on each vowel. In order to achieve this, the tongue must remain flexible: the tip and middle need to be strong and mobile, the root must be soft.

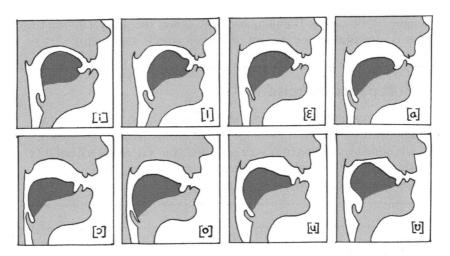

Figure 5.10: The position of the tongue on different vowels.

Each singer will have her favourite vowel or vowels. These tend to be ones where the tongue falls into a comfortable position and the formants are in tune with the fundamental frequency or pitch of the note. For more information on formants, see p. 119. It is often most effective to work on exercises with the best vowels and gradually move through onto the less comfortable ones.

Vowel exercise

Sing a series of separated notes, forming a slow ascending scale with a vowel change on each note. Then come down the scale in reverse. This is most useful when there is a gradual progression between the vowel shapes. Sing the separated notes as before, but move from the same vowel (e.g. [i]) to each of the others in turn. Then change the initial vowel and move from this to each of the others in turn. The aim is to sing a clear, unambiguous vowel on each note, but retain the intrinsic vocal timbre as you do so.

Figure 5.11: Vowel exercise.

There is a close relationship between [i] and [u], they both have a high tongue position. There is a similarly close relationship between [ɛ] and [ɔ]. This can be used in exercises that link these vowels, you can use one to help out a problem with the other.

When moving to higher pitches, the vowel may need to be modified in order to maintain a rich and balanced tone quality. The most effective way to achieve this is to aim to maintain the mouth and tongue position for a pure vowel sound. Extra space can be found in the pharynx, maybe with some extra soft-palate lift, or a widening or smiling sensation behind the palate or the nose. As well as this, the jaw will need to release slightly for higher pitches. This is most effective if the space between the back teeth is opened slightly, rather than the visible front teeth opening. There will be an element of both, of course, but the back release will be less likely to include a forward movement of the jaw.

Flexibility is again the key to achieving this modification. If the mouth is moved to a 'position', the vowel will sound less realistic than if the mouth is allowed to adapt and then return to its original form. If the singer keeps the *idea* of a vowel in place, even though the actual sound to the listener may be more neutral, the singer will then return to a pure vowel sound as the pitch lowers and the listener will believe that she has heard the true vowel throughout. There is more information on vowel modification on p. 120.

Vowel problems

Vowel problems, including an unclear vowel, a change of tone on particular vowels, or altered pitch on a particular vowel, may be caused by issues with the tongue, soft palate, jaw or pharyngeal constriction. In order to identify where the problem may be, check to see if the same problem exists on all vowels, or just some. Does the problem exist at all pitches? Try moving from a good vowel to the troublesome one, or move from the vowel on an easy pitch to the pitch that is problematic. Does a change of vowel make the note out of tune? Try to ascertain which element of the system (tongue body, tongue root, jaw, palate or pharynx) may be responsible for the problem. If you can't spot it easily, just try working on each in turn.

Consonants

These are made by constrictions in the vocal tract. They can be fricatives (the ones which buzz): 'v', 'z', 'j' or 'th' (voiced), or 'f', 's', 'sh' or 'th' (unvoiced). Another group are the plosives (air is trapped and then released which creates the sound); these also come in voiced/unvoiced pairings: 'b'/'p', 'd'/'t' and 'g'/'c'. Finally we have the liquid type of consonant: 'l' and 'r', and the nasal 'm', 'n' and 'ng'. In clear, effective singing or speaking, the consonants will be part of the flow of sound, rather than obstacles in the way.

Consonant exercise

Return to Breathing exercise 2. When you have recalled the flexibility of the belly used for the rhythmic hisses and buzzes of this exercise, extend this to plosives such as 'ba, ba, ba'. Feel the movement of the belly for each consonant: there will even be some slight movement for the quickest sounds. Now try extending this onto spoken phrases such as 'Humpty Dumpty sat on a wall'. For this you can feel the rhythm of the phrase in the belly. If you can then take this approach into singing, it will help the consonants to be clear and energised without compromising the airflow and legato line of the vowels.

Consonant problems

These fall into three main groups: speech defects, speech inefficiencies (e.g. tongue blade articulation) and weak or lazy articulation. Speech defects include lisps, consonant substitutions (e.g. 'f' for 'th') and distortions like the weak 'r'. These normally sort themselves out by the age of 8. If they don't, a speech therapist will be able to help. Therapy is in stages. First, the child is given exercises to strengthen the tongue tip and to ensure that the jaw and tongue have the right balance of use. Then the new speech sound is taught. These are incorporated into meaningless babble exercises that encourage repetition. When the motor skills are established, the sound can be incorporated into words and then into everyday speech.

Some speech patterns are part of the child's dialect and cultural identity. It is absolutely possible to alter usage within the context of singing whilst the child retains the speech pattern and usage related to his home and culture.

It is often the case that the jaw tries to help the tongue. The jaw may be seen to move forward for certain consonants (often for sibilants), or it may move up and down on repeated tongue movements (e.g. ya ya ya). In this case the jaw needs to be kept out of the picture while the action of the tongue is worked on (see Jaw exercise and Tongue and jaw exercise). If necessary the exercises can be carried out while the back teeth are gently closing on each other, or if the singer gently puts a finger between the back teeth.

The lips and facial expression

The muscles of facial expression are numerous and inter-related. When isolating various actions of the face, it is difficult to separate these from the emotion that goes with it, which in turn automatically brings in other facial actions. Our bodies are programmed to reflect sincere emotional feelings in the face. As a general guide, facial expression must be a natural result of communicating the meaning of a song; anything else will just get in the way. We don't want to see the workings of technique in a singer's face.

Common idiosyncratic expressions include:

- Frowning when concentrating.
- Raising the eyebrows when trying to 'lift' the sound.

- Smiling to the point of grimacing in an attempt to 'brighten' the sound.
- Tightening the lips to 'control' the sound.
- Letting the eyes drop or look to the sky when the eyes should be the prime channels of communication through which the singer carries the intention of the song.

None of these would aid with the expression of the spoken word and so they have no place in the expression of the sung word. Some gentle self-massage whilst singing can help to release unnecessary tension in the face.

5.5 From Mozart to musical theatre, gospel to pop: cross-training for the voice

Now that the voice is functioning well, you can address issues of musical style. Essentially, most elements of efficient voice production are the same for any vocal style. The differences will be in the subtleties of use. Children will imitate very effectively singers they have heard; so it is useful for the teacher to listen to the original track, in order to hear what they are trying to copy. Then you can make suggestions based on what children's voices can and can't do, compared with adult ones. In Contemporary Commercial Music (CCM) styles, speech quality will be extended higher into the vocal range, sometimes as high as F5 (although this is an extreme and few voices will be able to do this). In classical singing the shift is much lower, somewhere between C4 and G4.

Articulatory patterns will differ as the projected consonants used in classical repertoire will not be appropriate for pop. Consider the phrase 'Button up your overcoat'. Say this with the projected style of the classical singer, the 'tt' in button will fire out, the 'p' in up will do likewise. The second syllable in button will have a recognisable vowel sound. Now say it in a relaxed, American-style voice. The 'tt' becomes a soft 'd' sound, the second syllable of button is just a 'n'. In other examples, the [u] vowel will alter – for contemporary styles, this is made with the tongue further forward in the mouth, closer to our spoken [u] vowel.

Most children want to sing in a variety of styles, and this can be compared with cross-training for athletes. A runner will be encouraged to swim or cycle, and footballers have been known to do ballet. Children who are used to singing in thick-fold (chest) may be weak in the upper register, children used to singing in the upper register may be weak in speech range. It is important for the pupil to use all parts of their voice in a lesson. Dancers use all of their bodies, so why should a singer only use the upper vocal register, for example? Use mix-and-match exercises, especially over the range where it is possible to use either voice quality.

Register-bridging exercise or 4x4s

Starting on a note at the bottom of your range, sing an ascending scale to [a] with the first four notes in speech or chest quality and the next four notes in head or thin-fold. Come back down singing the first four in head and the next four in chest. Move up a semitone and repeat. Move this gradually up through your range, making sure that you don't over-weight the speech/chest on the higher pitches. You will find that there is a large pitch range where either register is possible

---

Resonance-bridging exercise: The wicked witch meets the cowardly lion
(thank you Robert Edwin for these)

On a descending five-note diatonic scale, try to sound like the wicked witch in *The Wizard of Oz* using a 'heh, heh, heh, heh, heh' lyric. It should be a highly nasalised sound created by lowering the soft palate and narrowing the rest of the resonance space. No exercise should be done passively without emotional support, so really 'get into it' with witchy finger pointing and the right sort of body language.

Next, find your cowardly lion voice. This time the lyric is a very woofy and heavy, 'ho, ho, ho, ho, ho'. The soft palate is up, the pharynx is wide, and the larynx is down. These are fun sounds, not pretty sounds, and they stretch the muscles as well as the mind.

Finally, you've sent your witch and lion off for singing lessons. Sing the 'heh' and 'ho' lyrics again with a new, more balanced sound. The extremes brought into the middle can create a very dynamic resonance spectrum. Be sure to do the exercise in *both* registers.

It is important to note the similarities between healthy vocal technique for adults and children, and the similarities between healthy techniques for different musical styles. There is much more similarity than difference. Keep returning to the basics of posture, breathing, release in the face and jaw, keeping the system balanced, poised and ready to go!

Chapter 5 Summary

Posture:

- Good posture requires balance, a state of alert poise, where the head is directed up.
- Bad habits may involve pulling the head forward or pulling the chin up.
- Good alignment is a direction, not a position.

Breathing:

- Effective breathing uses the lower abdominal muscles.
- Feel them moving in gradually as you sing and then releasing for the air to fall into the body.
- Use hissing and buzzing exercises to feel the movement of these muscles.
- Feel the response of the muscles in the waist, they will engage as you breathe out.
- The back muscles may be used in young adult singers, but only for occasional vocal extremes.
- The singer will not be aware of any work in the diaphragm during singing.

The larynx:

- The larynx is primarily a valve, it is very good at lifting and squeezing shut.
- It contains the vocal folds, when these vibrate they are the source of the sound.
- Pitch is determined by the length and tension in the vocal folds.
- Loudness is determined by the force of collision of the vocal folds.
- Vocal timbre and voice register can be determined by the thickness of the vocal folds. Speech quality, in the lower pitch range, is made with thicker vocal folds.
- Vibrato is a natural phenomenon that can be heard in adolescent and young adult voices. All voices are capable of making a wobble that may sound similar to vibrato.
- The larynx will have a tendency to constrict, this can be heard as a degree of harshness in the sound.

- There are four types of onset: aspirate, glottal, simultaneous or creak. The first three are all commonly used in many styles of singing.
- Breathiness is caused by air escaping between the vocal folds. It can be as a result of poor coordination of the laryngeal muscles, slight inflammation of the vocal folds or just as a result of bad habits.
- Belting is an extreme vocal gesture. It is only to be used sparingly and must be taught carefully.

The vocal tract:

- The length of the vocal tract is determined by the height of the larynx and the position of the lips.
- The soft palate must be raised if the sound is not to be nasal.
- Yawning and swallowing are frequent habitual actions that conflict with good singing.
- The pharynx is a squeezy tube: the constrictions and openings along its length give the sound its qualities, including all the vowels and consonants.
- The tongue needs to be flexible in order to articulate text clearly, the tongue root must not be tense or pressed onto the larynx.
- The jaw needs to be released but not over-opened.
- Projected resonance may feel like vibrations across the front of the face or the roof of the mouth.
- Vowels are made by the position of the tongue and, to some extent, the lips.
- Problems with consonants can nearly always be addressed with the right approach, this may be from a qualified speech therapist.
- The expressions of the face should be as a direct consequence of the emotions of the song, we don't want to see technique in the face.

Different musical styles:

- Children may want to sing music from a variety of styles.
- Most CCM singing is based on speech, taking speech quality to higher pitches and using a speech-style articulation of text.

Interlude E

Vocal tract acoustics – resonance and formants

The sound source – the larynx

The pitch of the voice, whether we perceive it as high or low, is measured as fundamental frequency. This is the number of events (disturbances, collisions, vibrations) per second. The pitch A4 has a frequency of 440 Hertz (Hz); vocal folds producing this pitch will be colliding 440 times per second. The vibrating frequency of an object is determined by its mass, length and tension. Vocal folds will vibrate at a higher frequency range if they are thinner (longer), or tighter.

The loudness of the voice is referred to as amplitude (the size of the sound pressure change) or sound pressure level (SPL), which is measured in decibels (dB). Vocal folds colliding with a greater movement at the midline of the glottis will produce sound of greater amplitude (produced by higher subglottic air pressure and a greater rapidity of vocal fold closure).

All pitched or periodic vocal sounds (with a regular fundamental frequency) will have harmonics (these are the additional vibrating frequencies in the harmonic series). Harmonics at some frequencies are stronger than others; this gives the sound its unique timbre. A4 on an oboe is recognisably different from A4 on a violin, A4 sung by a tenor has a different timbre from A4 sung by a soprano. So, how does this happen? How can vibrating vocal folds produce sounds with different timbres? The distribution of the harmonics will be affected by how rapidly the vocal folds snap together; it will also be affected by the movement of the mucosal wave across the vocal fold. Speech quality, thin-fold or head voice and falsetto all have different vibratory patterns across the vocal fold and as a result they generate a different distribution of harmonics in the sound.

The amplification system – the pharynx

The sound energy leaving the larynx, with its own family of harmonic distribution, passes into the vocal tract. This is a tube with an almost infinitely variable shape.

The cavities and constrictions formed by the height of the larynx, position of the pharynx wall, tongue, soft palate and jaw will create smaller spaces, each with their own formant frequency. This is a resonant phenomenon meaning that a particular group of frequencies will be amplified within this space. Any hollow chamber has a formant frequency: an open-topped bottle will have a variable resonant frequency depending on how much fluid is in it, and how much air remains. The formant frequency of an open-topped bottle will also depend on the width of the opening, this has relevance for jaw opening at different pitches in singers. The vocal tract has the ability to form more than one cavity within it, enabling a number of formants to be amplified on any given note or vowel. If one of these spaces corresponds exactly with a group of harmonics from the original sound, this aspect of the sound will be boosted and we will hear more of this group of harmonics. A singer will be working with up to five audible formants. The first two formants will determine the vowel and the next three will determine vocal quality or timbre.

For example, in an [i] vowel we hear more high (and bright) harmonics than in an [u] vowel (which sounds darker). The first two formants, or groups of harmonics in the voice, will determine the vowel sound. The unique quality of the vowel will be due to whether the harmonics boosted are relatively high or relatively low. When we look at the pattern of the formants on different vowel sounds, and we know the position of the tongue for each of them, we can deduce that certain tongue positions will boost certain frequencies.

The chart opposite shows that vowels with a high tongue position, [i] and [u], have a low F1; [æ] and [ɑ] have a higher F1. Vowels with a forward tongue position, [i] and [y], have a high F2. Vowels with a backed tongue position, [ɔ] and [ɑ] have a low F2. As the tongue moves from raised to flattened the F1 rises; as the tongue moves forward within the mouth, the F2 rises.

For a vowel to be sung at a particular frequency, the resonators need to reinforce a sound that has partials of the fundamental and also partials within both vowel formants. The vowel formants have to be altered to accommodate the harmonic series. Articulators need to remain flexible and responsive so that they can instinctively seek the position for the best resonance for each vowel and each pitch.

If the resonators are 'out of tune' with the harmonics, the sound may be dulled or the fundamental pitch may appear to be out of tune. Alternatively the singer may mis-tune the formants, giving the singer the impression (due to the selective nature of the internal conduction of the sound) that the fundamental is in tune when in fact, it is not.

When the singer is above G5, clear text is not possible. This is because in many of the vowels the first formant is actually lower than the fundamental frequency. The vowels [a], [æ] and [ʌ] are the only ones which have first formant frequency above F5. Most composers have been aware of this limitation and it is rare to find crucial parts of the text set at high pitches.

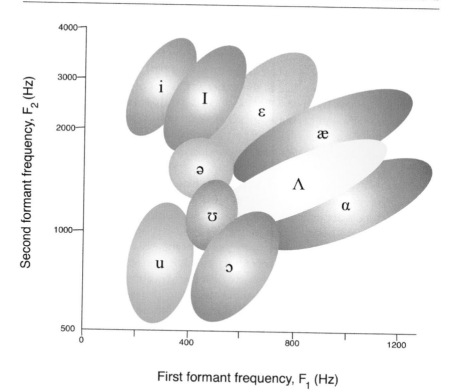

Figure E1: The British English vowel formants.

More advanced singers may benefit from some conscious vowel modification when approaching the upper passaggio, or register change. The vowels [ɑ], [œ], [ɔ], and [U] will benefit from moving towards a darker [o]. The vowels [ɛ], [I], [e] and [i] will benefit from moving towards an [y]. This helps the singer to tune in the upper formants that contribute to the ringing quality described below. Another useful by-product of this vowel modification can be the reduction in breathiness. When the singer uses the more closed vowel colours in the upper range, the enhanced 'ring' (upper frequencies) in the sound ensures that the vocal folds come together without an audible escape of air (breathiness). The activity in the vocal tract has a direct effect on the behaviour of the vocal folds.

Twang, ring or the singer's formant

A trained singer or speaker can learn to enhance the frequencies in the level near 3 kHz in the spectrum, 2–4 octaves above the sung pitch. This particular band of frequencies is extremely useful to the singer as it is not present as a peak in the orchestral spectrum. This means that the singer can be heard above the sound of an orchestra, even though, of course, an orchestra is much louder than the singer. The singer's formant cuts through the orchestral texture, carrying the voice.

There are many explanations for how and where we produce the singer's formant. It is one of the areas in which world experts in voice cannot quite agree! It is likely that the singer's formant has something to do with the dimensions of the epilarynx, or the tiny tube between the vocal folds and the top of the larynx. The larynx tube is about 2cm long in an adult. It is bordered on the bottom by the vocal folds, on the posterior wall by the arytenoid cartilages and on the anterior wall by the epiglottis. The resonant frequency of the epilarynx corresponds with the resonant frequency of the upper formants. This is then amplified by a combination of the wider opening of the pharynx directly above the larynx, coupled with a narrowing of the pharyngeal wall above this. As an interesting point to note, the dimensions of the epilarynx are almost identical to those of the outer ear canal. This particular resonant frequency produced by the human voice will be picked up clearly and loudly by the human ear.

Singing louder than the orchestra...

In highly trained children's voices we can see a similar boost in the frequency spectrum, but this occurs at slightly higher frequencies (nearer to 4kHz). We know that the epilarynx is proportionally smaller in children, and its resonant frequency corresponds exactly with the singer's formant in children's voices.

Chapter 6

Structuring lessons and practice

'Always desire to learn something useful'. Sophocles

Whether you are working with a group or teaching individual singers, and whether those singers are children or adults, the importance of structure and planning is just as valid. The goal may be a performance or an assessment, or it may be learning a particular song. It is helpful to have a goal, rather than just 'learning to sing better'; even if this goal is performing to the next pupil arriving for a lesson. Between the start of lessons/rehearsals to the end goal, there is micro and macro planning. Each lesson needs an overall structure, and the lessons themselves should lead progressively towards the performance.

6.1 Individual lesson structure

The initial conversation is useful to tune into the physical and emotional well-being of the pupil. In the first lesson this conversation may take some time, as you will be forming a picture of the pupil's background. You may ask:

- What kind of singing do you do now – at home, at school, at choir?
- Do you play any other instruments – if so for how long and to what level?
- What other things are you good at – sport, dance, acting, chess?
- Does anyone else in your family sing?

You will also need to ask relevant questions about health and injuries.

- Have you ever visited a doctor about your voice?

- Have you had any significant injuries or operations that may affect your posture or breathing (for example, back or neck injuries)?
- Do you have any recurrent health issues that may affect your voice or your energy levels (asthma, bronchitis, post-viral fatigue)?
- Do you have any special help at school? (This can tell you if the child has any special educational needs.)

If this is a regular pupil the questions may be:

- How has your week been?
- Did your football match/school concert/brother's party/maths exam go OK?
- How was your practice?
- Did you manage to memorise the song I suggested?

During this time you will be assessing the health of his speaking voice, listening for breathiness, harshness, cracking or weakness. You will be observing his breathing, watching for even movements in the body. You will be looking at his posture for signs of holding or collapsing. You will be reading his body language to see if he is defensive, unsure, anxious, embarrassed, over-enthusiastic or tired. The sub-text of this assessment is probably more useful than the actual answers given.

This initial assessment will determine the content and pace of the lesson. A good singing lesson will:

- follow a basic structure: warm-up, exercises, repertoire
- include sight-reading, theory and aural training: these can be integrated into the other elements of the lesson most of the time
- integrate the body, mind and voice: physical embodiment of the singing process linked with imagination, understanding and communication
- present one or at most two new ideas on which to work: communicate this clearly to the pupil so that they know how to practise it
- send the pupil away in better voice than at the start (the speaking voice will be clearer and brighter) and in a more positive frame of mind. Pupils have to know that singing (and this includes practice at home) will make them feel better in themselves.

After this initial assessment you will begin to warm-up the voice, the theory of which is explored below. This systematic approach is important for individual lessons, group rehearsals and for individual private practice. There is a noticeable similarity between these structures, which is fully intentional. The difference is that, within the lesson or rehearsal, the teacher will respond to the sound and vary the approach accordingly. Eventually, the pupil will learn to do this for herself in her practice; although it is arguable that all singers need some sort of expert guidance throughout their performing lives.

Physical and emotional empathy

As you are teaching, you may well feel a physical empathy with the pupil. If he has a gripped mid-abdomen, you may feel this in your own body. This is a useful tool for diagnosis, although it can be exhausting if you are picking up on too much unnecessary tension. Remember that this physical mirroring is two-way. You can often influence the behaviour of your pupils by consciously relaxing in your own body the part you perceive as tense in theirs. If their speaking voice is brittle, you can soften yours. If they have a collapsed head and neck alignment, ensure that your own is directed up.

Remember that this physical mirroring is two way.

Hands-on assessment and guidance is extremely useful, a small gesture can replace hundreds of words. There are many ethical considerations with this issue: these are dealt with in more detail in the section on **child protection** (Interlude F, p. 147). Between adults, it is a mutual consent: adults will let you know, either verbally or physically, if they are not happy with hands-on contact. With the younger pupil it is advisable to use common sense and caution. When teenagers are in the midst of adolescent turmoil, physical contact can sometimes be counter-productive.

If you are having the sort of conversation with your pupils outlined at the beginning of this chapter, it is likely that they may tell you about problems or upsets in their life. How to manage this is again a matter of common sense and caution. Remember that you are there to teach him singing, not to counsel him or solve his problems. This is also dealt with in more detail in the section on child protection.

You are not there to counsel them or solve their problems.

Notebooks and recordings

It is good practice for the teacher to keep a written note of every lesson. In this way you can monitor progress, ensuring that you are covering the right ground and that you are not repeating more than is necessary. It is useful for the pupil to have a notebook in which to write what needs to be worked on. If the parent sits in on the lesson, he or she can take notes. The role of parents in lessons has been discussed in previous chapters.

Some teachers make an audio or even a video recording of each lesson. This is an extremely useful tool for the pupils. If they can listen to the lesson when they get home, they can not only make notes of what worked and what didn't, they can also hear the work in progress much more effectively from the outside. A recording is useful for the teacher as a very good way of assessing progress over time. It is also evidence of what took place, should there be any future misunderstandings about the behaviour of either the teacher or the pupil.

Listening through to a recording of a lesson you have given is a valuable means of self-assessment. If you have the time and patience, make a note of how much time was spent on:

- the teacher giving instruction
- the teacher demonstrating
- the teacher chatting/reminiscing/recalling anecdotes
- the pupil speaking – conversation relevant to the work in progress
- the pupil speaking – general chat
- the pupil singing specific passages/exercises
- the pupil singing through longer sections, uninterrupted.

There need not be a rule for how much time is spent on each activity, but this sort of self-evaluation can be a salutary means of reflection on one's teaching practice.

6.2 Physical skills: athletes' training principles

As music teachers, we are responsible for teaching aural, reading, interpretive and stylistic skills; these areas are already addressed in many excellent books on music teaching. As this book is dealing specifically with singing, it might be useful to take a look at the process of training a physical skill. The field of sports science is generally ahead of music, so we can see how its theory of training can apply to us.

Training ensures that the muscles can work more quickly and efficiently, delaying fatigue, increasing duration and limiting injury. The muscles that we are training are the larger muscles related to posture and breathing, as well as the smaller muscles within the larynx and vocal tract. Some of these groups are in frequent daily use, for example, the diaphragm, the tongue and jaw and the muscles responsible for lower pitches in the voice. Others will need to be 'woken from cold'; for example, those responsible for high pitches within the voice. The muscles responsible for swallowing will need to be reminded of a completely different scheme of coordination.

These headings are from sports research; the interpretation is for singing.

Training must be specific

Exercises need to be tailored to the specific needs of the current repertoire. For example, this may involve: coloratura runs, high range dramatic, high range quiet, mid-range speech quality, mid-high range belt, low larynx twang, or high larynx twang. Whatever challenges the repertoire presents, these should be reflected in the nature of the exercises used in the pupil's lesson and practice.

Overload the system

In order to improve, you need to work slightly harder than usual. This is in terms of frequency, intensity, duration and type. Intensity, in this instance, is referring to the power and strength of the voice, not just the loudness. It is the most effective parameter for increasing performance. This refers more to general stamina than to specific extreme demands. A performer preparing for a demanding operatic role, for example, will have a rehearsal period where she has to work for many more hours in the day than on a performance day. This overloading helps the singer to improve and build stamina.

Train progressively

Gradually increase the workload. Vocal loading (see **vocal health**, Chapter 7) is related to intensity (loudness), time (how long you are voicing) and emotional stress. The first two of these you have direct control over, the third you can be aware of. Pace your practice to increase the length of sessions and intensity of singing incrementally. No sudden surprises.

Balance hard and easy training

High-impact vocalising leads to local injury of tissues that need time to repair. Short and frequent rests are vital, or use periods of low-impact singing to give the larynx time to recover. These times may be used for memorising notes or text quietly, speaking through the text, or singing gently down an octave.

Vary the training

Use different exercises from time to time. Include several pieces in your practice repertoire so you can have a different focus from day to day.

Train regularly

Practise at least five days out of every seven. If you practise less than three times a week, you are unlikely to make significant progress. If you have more than two weeks without practice (for example during a trip away) your voice will have forgotten some technique and you will have to go back a step or two.

Rest

Resting with a different activity is more beneficial than passive resting. The science behind this has shown that the neurological systems in the brain recover from fatigue more quickly if they have an inflow of activity from non-fatigued parts of the body. For young singers, this complementary activity is often sport or dance. It can be playing another musical instrument, for example playing through piano accompaniments.

Resting with a different activity is more beneficial than passive resting.

Muscular fitness is different from habitual muscle memory. Assuming that as a child you learnt to ride a bicycle (most likely with much patience and help from a parent at the time), as an adult you can probably get onto a bicycle and ride it without falling off, even if you have not ridden one for ten or more years. However, you may not, after ten years, be fit enough to cycle for 20 miles on your first outing. The same applies to singing. You may have learnt an aria last year, but after some time away from it, the aria won't be ready to perform unless you have spent some time working the piece back into the voice.

6.3 Warm-ups: why are they necessary and how do we do them?

Introduction

Warming up for any physical activity is essential to prevent injury, to reinforce good habits and to focus the mind and body on the matter in hand. Going through the ritual of a warm-up at the start of each rehearsal or lesson can bring the members of the group together and give them a

common purpose. On a physical level we are aiming to get ease and range of motion as well as eliminating tension; a gentle and systematic warm-up will get the body and mind ready for the more demanding and athletic activity of singing. This section will only give a few suggestions for specific warm-up exercises as there are many of these already published elsewhere. It will mainly provide a theoretical framework within which you can structure your own warm-up to meet the needs of your singers and to maximise the time available to you.

The theory behind warming-up

All warm-up exercises need to have a direct relationship to singing; they are not just 'for fun'. In other words, if you don't know exactly what the exercise is achieving, leave it out. In order to understand the purpose of warm-ups, it can help again to look at findings in sports science. Musical performance, like athletic performance, involves prolonged, highly controlled and sometimes forceful activity. The demands that this makes on the body can be variable but in all cases they combine speed, strength and duration.

Muscles need energy in order to work. This energy comes from the metabolic process of converting substances derived from nutrients, some of which are stored in the cell and some which need to be transported in the blood. The initial few seconds of activity is an anaerobic process – this relies on the cell's glycogen reserves and results in the production of lactic acid. Prolonged anaerobic activity can result in a build-up of lactic acid, which is effectively a toxin and after some time, will impair performance. Aerobic activity, which starts after several seconds of gentle activity, requires a balance between oxygen availability and its use by the muscle.

The process of converting nutrients into muscle power causes a rise in temperature: the muscles are literally warming up. This dilates the capillary beds and increases blood flow to the muscle; it also aids other metabolic functions such as enzyme activity. The rise in temperature will also mean that the connective tissues and fluids are less viscous, enabling easier and quicker movements. The muscle itself is looser and more pliable, this is an important consideration when the vibrating muscle (*vocalis* and *thyro-arytenoid*) is the source of the sound.

Applying low-intensity exercise to muscles for a few minutes will mean that the muscles will work more effectively.

Different sporting activities need different ways of preparing. A half-hour morning jog does not need much warming up beforehand, as this will happen during the run. The important thing for this runner is to stretch and warm-down at the end. If, however, the athlete is to play rugby or squash, this demands quick and varied movements, including moments of extreme exertion. For these sports athletes are advised to begin training with a 10–15 minute all-over body activity such as jogging or skipping. This should be followed with particular stretching exercises before moving onto the more demanding parts of training. The varied physical activity needed in the more demanding sports is more like singing, which involves big gestures such as loud high notes, quick and varied movements such as fast runs as well as the gentler mid-range, mid-dynamic equivalent of jogging.

As well as improving metabolic activity within the muscle cells, we also need to encourage flexibility of the muscles and of the connective tissues. Once the muscles are basically warm, gentle stretching through-out the range of the muscles in question will overcome stiffness and limited movement. Muscles that have been contracted over time, with-out a follow-up stretch, can remain in a shortened position. This can be a problem in postural muscles where habitual shortening can result in limited movement. Muscle shortening can also result in an imbalance of activity between related muscle groups where one is over-contracting and another is under-working. This is often the cause of lower back pain where the different sets of postural muscles have become out of balance with each other. When stretching, it is important not to stretch too much, as this may cause injury. All that is needed is a gentle movement, allowing the muscle to lengthen rather than forcing it to.

Once we have achieved flexibility we can go on to technical exercises that will help to develop muscular coordination, so the interacting muscles can change positions smoothly. They will also develop muscular strength: the ability to exert a force for a brief interval. This is important for high-impact singing without injury.

With reference to singing, we can divide the muscle groups into specific areas of the body, before bringing them all back together again. As well as warming up muscles we are encouraging good habits of voice use. The warm-up can be used as a place in which to introduce and work on vocal technique.

Intensity of performance, speed of movement and length of performance can cause muscle fatigue. In simple terms, this means anything loud, high, fast or long. Singing intensely without prior preparation will exhaust nutrient reserves within the muscles and diminish performance. This will result in muscle fatigue and rest will be needed for recovery. Recovery is most effective with active rest; pursuing a different activity rather than inactivity. This can be incorporated into the warm-up or practice routine. The diverting activity produces a flow of impulses from the non-fatigued parts of the body, this shifts the brain functioning from inhibition to facilitation.

Finally, the singer is bringing the activity of singing to the forefront of attention, allowing focus on one activity. In a choir, we are bringing together individual singers to work as a unit with one common aim. This psychological aspect is a by-product of the physiological warm-up, both on an individual and a group level, helping the singers to get the most effective results and the maximum enjoyment from their singing.

A good warm-up will have a seamless flow from one section to the next: the leader or teacher will respond at each stage to the sound of the individual or the group, with direction to address their particular needs. By the end of the warm-up, the singer should have his voice ready to begin singing any of his repertoire.

The framework for a warm-up

Wake up and balance the body

First, encourage a calm stillness in the singer. If you are warming-up a group, they will have all come from different activities and will have different energy levels.

When your singers are quiet and focused they need to warm-up the muscles of the torso. This can be gentle running on the spot, some arm circling, a bit of dancing. What you do will depend on the age of your singers and the physical space you have available. Once the body has moved gently in order to give the muscles a basic warm-up, it is then useful to stretch the larger muscles of the torso with some sideways and forward bending. With all stretching and bending, it is the quality of the movement that is more important than the extent of movement: keep breathing throughout the stretch. Try not to let the singers think of the stretches as a competition, even if it is with themselves! Stretching should always be within a comfortable range, not an extreme action. Once you have done this gentle stretching, move on to releasing tension in the neck, shoulders and jaw. This can be with massage, yawning, gentle neck stretches (don't do circling of the head, this can cause strain or injury, keep it to sideways and up-and-down stretches), shoulder circling, shoulder scrunches. Encourage your singers to feel the release as a result of the stretch.

When the body is warm and stretched, you can remind the singers of their posture. Good posture is vital to enable efficient voice use. Any imbalance in the alignment of the body will result in unnecessary muscle tension and inefficient use. Aim for an alert stillness; if in doubt, refer to the principles of the Alexander Technique. Check that the weight is evenly balanced over the toes and heels, releasing the knees. Look at the relationship between the head, shoulders, hips, knees and feet – could you drop a line down through the middle of all of them? It is often helpful to go to a place of bad alignment and then release into a more comfortable one. Muscular release will be more effective with light movements and touch than with energetic or extreme ones.

Breathing

Theory

The most effective focus for breathing movement in the singer is the lower abdominal or belly region. It is important to exercise this area, whilst remaining stable elsewhere. Breath flow for singing does not need to be pushed, but it does need careful coordination. Breathing exercises need to remind the singer of the area for attention. You can then work on reducing the effort levels in this region.

Practice

Get the singers to put their hands on their bellies to feel the movement *in* as they sing and *out* as they breathe in. If they get confused with ins and outs, think of the belly like a balloon – if it's got air in, it will be fatter; if you are singing, air is going out and the balloon is getting smaller.

Use 'shh', 'ff' or 'ss' to feel this movement. Then put sound behind these and use 'vv', 'zz' or 'jj'. If possible use rolled 'rr' and 'brr' (the lip trill, or horse noise!). Feel the tummy moving inwards as the air leaves the lungs. This is more of a slow 'zipping up' than a kick. Let go of these muscles without collapsing or lifting anywhere else and the air will rush in – you don't need to suck air in. Now try this to short repeated hisses or shushes and feel the flexibility of these muscles. The belly muscles should feel like wobbly jelly: movement is more important than effort.

Release the throat

Theory

The prime function of the larynx is as a valve: the larynx is designed to lift and squeeze very effectively every time we swallow. This reflex is very powerful; the tendency to constrict can arise as a result of anxiety, over-working, or just an unfamiliar sensation. When we sing or speak, we need to keep this part of the system released and open. A tight sound can be caused by constriction in the larynx, or further up the throat in the pharynx, or it can be due to tongue tension. These are all related to the swallowing reflex: if in doubt, work to release all of them. A constricted larynx will sound harsh, scratchy or cracked. A constricted pharynx will sound tight and squeezed, like Mr Bean or Kermit the Frog. If the back of the tongue is tense, the larynx is not free to move, the sound is hard and can sound pressed or hooty. The whole throat itself is a very flexible tube. It is not possible to 'open the throat' entirely; the nearest sensation we have to this is the yawn, which brings with it the most extreme tongue root tension and is largely inappropriate for singing. Instead, focus on specific areas such as laryngeal deconstriction and tongue root release and the rest will follow.

Practice

Breathe in as if you have just had a happy surprise (e.g. winning the lottery). Then do this silently. Then put your hands over your ears and do the same, aim to make no noise at all as you inhale. Laugh out loud, then imagine a silent giggle or smile in your throat. Now consciously open from a neutral position into this wider, laughing feeling and return to neutral (this wide, laughing feeling is not to be confused with the deep feeling of a yawn). Try imitating ape noises and movement (it always brings a giggle) then moving into sound maintaining the feeling of looseness. Sing through partly closed lips (not the nose), allowing the cheeks to puff out; this will encourage deconstriction. The muscles of the face and lips are soft, the sound is gentle.

Warm-up the larynx

Theory

These exercises should use and stretch the muscles, working throughout the pitch range. They will also address voice qualities originating within the larynx, such as breathiness, harshness and register-bridging. Warming-up the larynx includes work on onset: breathy, glottal or simultaneous. As the vocal folds are working through their full range of movement, they are loosening any sticky phlegm on the surface. This will then dissipate with a swallow. Always start quietly in the lower middle of the range, and then extend the pitch up and down.

Practice

Slide up and down on small intervals, no more than a fifth, to 'ng' as in 'sing' not 'song', as this brings the tongue further forward and away from the top of the larynx. Gradually move to higher and lower pitches. Try using less breath while keeping the sound clear and mobile, and extend the pitch range of each siren. As you extend the pitch range, move freely between speech quality and thin-fold (girls) or falsetto (boys), sliding off the sung sound at the bottom. Open onto vowels with vocalised sighing, staying quiet: move from 'ng' to 'ee', then through 'eh', 'ah', 'oh' and 'oo'. Do the same sliding exercises on voiced fricatives ('vv', 'jj' [as in regime], 'zz'). If possible, then move on to a rolled 'r' or a lip trill (horse or motorbike noises), all the time sliding and not fixing the pitch.

The start of the sound (onset) on an open vowel can be glottal, breathy or simultaneous. The latter is the best for everyday use; the others are for special effects. Practise a gentle glottal onset followed by a breathy one, then imagine the 'h' and sing a series of short 'ah's using virtually no air.

Explore resonance

Theory

This covers voice qualities dependent on the set-up of the vocal tract, such as voice projection, larynx lowering/raising, soft palate raising and pharyngeal widening/narrowing.

Voice projection tends to rely on developing 'twangy' or 'ringing' sounds. Larynx lowering (for richer qualities) should not use any tongue root activity; larynx raising is normally for brighter or speech-like qualities — musical theatre or pop. Soft palate raising reduces nasality and increases the resonant space. If in doubt hold the nose when singing: if this alters the sound quality, the palate is dropped.

Practice

Play with witchy noises and quacking, making sure that you are deconstricting (see 'Release the throat'). Then try this sensation with the resonance in the mouth and not the nose (a 'munchkin' sound). Sing whole phrases in this quality and feel the lack of effort required for a lot of noise. Loosen the jaw slightly, allow the larynx to drop, and you will soften the edges of the sound. You may feel vibration in the roof of your mouth or in the front of your face.

Feel that all of these exercises involve the least necessary effort; if in doubt, keep wiggling elsewhere in the body. Breathe in over an 'ee' vowel to raise the back of the tongue and release tongue root pressure. Feel the tongue root under the chin with the thumb: this should be soft and mobile.

Clarify articulation

Theory

This covers the singing of text. In general, make sure that all articulation is primarily with the tongue, not the jaw. Highly energised consonants are very useful for re-balancing muscle use and airflow. Try to sing through them rather than allowing them to stop the air.

Practice

Drop the jaw without pulling it forwards (feel the jaw hinge just in front of the ears), sing 'ya, ya, ya' exercises keeping the jaw loose but still. Touch the outer edge of the upper and lower lips with the tip of the tongue, without moving the jaw forward. Bite a knuckle and sing a phrase, drop the jaw, let the tongue hang out and do the same. Check the tongue position on all vowels; 'ee' has highest tongue with the sides of the tongue against the upper molars. Check that the tongue does not press back as it moves towards 'ah': there should still be a feeling of lift in the middle. As you move from 'ah' through 'oh' to 'oo', the change will be primarily by bringing the lips forward, although it is important not to overuse the lips. You may not feel movement of the tongue, even though it must be moving in order to change the vowel.

Practise tongue twisters to descending scales. Invent your own combinations.

Summary

It is important that none of these stages is missed out during a warm-up. If you have limited time, you can still move through all the stages but spend less time on them. If your singers are familiar with your methods, it only takes a word or a gesture and you can achieve a whole package of responses from them. It is quite possible to warm-up the voice ready to sing in about five minutes, especially if the voices are healthy and the singers have been awake for some time. If you are able to spend longer on your warm-up, it can be a valuable opportunity for developing group vocal technique. Allow your singers now to move from this place of warming-up into singing: there should be nothing different in the way they approach their repertoire.

6.4 Private practice

'What happens on the concert platform is a direct consequence of what happens in the practice room. There is no magic and no mystery: good practice results in good performances, faulty practice will produce poor performances.' Iznaola[49]

Motivation to practise

For those singers wishing to improve their singing either for performance or for assessment, regular practice is essential if the individual is to make progress. There are general guidelines for effective practice that apply to any skill acquisition. The practice must be regular; it must be systematic and structured. Goals should be clear from the outset of each practice session. It should involve tasks that use both memory and reading skills. It is also essential that the performer develops reflective self-assessment.

In order for the child to gain singing skills, expert tuition from an experienced specialist singing teacher is preferable. This does not rule out the great benefits of guidance from a more generalist musician such as a classroom teacher or a choir conductor. If the younger child is having regular individual singing lessons, the role of parents or carers in supervising daily singing practice is extremely valuable. Finally the influence of the child's peer group, especially for teenagers, is powerful and can be very effective for learning. For example, older children who form a band and rehearse regularly under no adult supervision will often achieve high-quality results. This has the added advantage of encouraging self-motivation and positive group identity for the adolescent.

This is a guide on effective practice. When you practise you should ideally go through each of these stages. It is important not to skip any of them, although you can choose to spend as long as you like on each one. Establishing a routine for this helps you to be mindful of the process as well as enabling you to build patterns of good habitual usage. Before you start, plan your practice, establishing your particular goals in advance. Plan how long you intend spending on each section; if you stray from your planned practice schedule make this a conscious choice, not just a result of a lack of mindfulness. Much of this structure is also covered in the section on warming-up; the theory behind both of them is similar.

Personal practice routine

Set up your mind

Focus on practising singing without any other distractions. Effective practice is often boring and repetitive, so it is important that you remain mindful of your actions. Emotional detachment from the activity is important in order to enable objective observation. Don't condemn yourself for mistakes: listen, observe, feel and respond.

Align your body

Remember the sensation of balanced posture: perhaps use tension and release methods to achieve this. Poise is mid-way between collapse and tension; keep exploring the point of balance between the two. Practise singing whilst standing up. If you are sitting at the piano to learn notes this is a different sort of learning process; technical practice is the reinforcement of good habits and is more effective in a good standing posture.

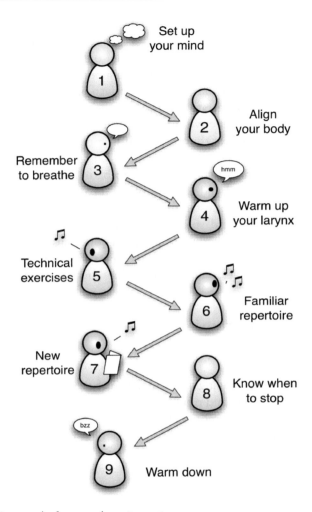

Figure 6.1: An example of a personal practice routine.

Remember to breathe

Use breathing exercises that apply release and engagement of the muscles in the lower abdomen, along with an open release in the upper body. Nothing is ever held at any time; the system, although stable, is always poised for action. Use repeated rhythms to encourage flexibility. Remember that the release on the in-breath enables you to welcome in the air, not allowing the system to collapse.

Warm up your larynx

This is gentle warming-up, not to be confused with technical exercises. It encourages systematic flexing and stretching of the muscles specific to singing, encouraging the flow of blood to these areas and reducing the likelihood of injury. It could include quiet sliding through the range, buzzing and humming.

Technical exercises

These are exercises for agility, articulation and resonance. They will include whatever your teacher is working on with you currently. They need to be applied systematically as part of your planned practice schedule.

Familiar repertoire

Use a piece you know you sing well to remind your body how to do it, establishing good habitual patterns.

New repertoire

Now you are ready to learn and work on new repertoire. Establish your goals before you start, work on small sections slowly and then build these into longer sections. Singing a whole piece from the beginning is practising a performance, not technical practice.

Know when to stop

When things are going well, it is tempting to 'ride the crest of the wave' and to carry on and on with singing. Plan ahead when you will take a break and stick to this regardless. You can always come back later to continue your practice.

Warm-down

Bring your larynx back to a more relaxed state ready for speaking, by buzzing or humming gently down to your lowest pitch range.

When things are going well it is tempting to ride the crest of a wave.

6.5 Memorisation of music

Performing from memory can have many benefits. First, if the singer is familiar with the song, she will have a deeper understanding of it. Second, the performer can 'inhabit' the music and the text, allowing it to flow uninhibited from the emotions. It has been suggested that this may have links with brain activity. Reading is a predominantly left-brain, decoding activity. If we are reading whilst singing, we are less able to access the right-brain, whole-picture, emotional aspect of a performance. A third benefit of performing from memory is that it allows the singer to have ongoing eye contact and communication with the audience. This enables the performance to be an interactive experience for both the performer and the audience.

No one likes to have to perform from memory. In the same way that no one wants to practise and no child wants to go to bed at night. It's amazing how many pupils think that they are alone in feeling uncomfortable about memorising songs. Once we have agreed that we all feel the same way, we can accept it and find ways of making the process easier. It can help if we have some basic understanding of how the brain remembers information in the first place.

Memory function can be conceptualised as three stores [50]. The first is the **sensory store**, receiving information from our environment. The sensory memory has a limited amount of storage and so any information from here to which we attach importance is then passed to the **short-term memory** store. This has a working memory in which we process information at a conscious level. This part of the memory is more stable and can retain musical phrases or lines of text while they are being repeated or worked on. If the repetitions are thoughtful and meaningful, the neural pathways will become stronger and the information will be retained. The working memory is the part that is used while we are sight-reading or improvising.

Information that has been passed to the **long-term memory** will remain if it is reinforced. Music that has been memorized by repetition for a day may remain for a week or so. Information repeated after a week may remain for a month, and so on. The long-term memory store is divided into three broad types of memory: procedural, semantic and episodic. **Procedural** memory will include the sequence of muscular actions to sing a particular melody or exercise, when to breathe, how to stand and so on. **Semantic** memory will inform us what that melody is; it will make the connections with the meaning of the text as we sing it. **Episodic** memory will link the song with associations of when we last sang it: for example, how we felt when we last went over it in a singing lesson.

Techniques for improving your memorisation skills

- Memory can be improved by different means. First, by having a healthy lifestyle. Eating a balanced diet, exercising frequently and limiting or eliminating drugs and alcohol. The teacher cannot assume that children will have regular meals. The pupil may skip breakfast, or not fancy what is on offer for lunch. This will have a significant effect on his concentration.
- Give full attention to the process of receiving the information. If you are memorising the line of a song, concentrate completely as you sing it through; focus on the feel of the text in your mouth, picture the

story in your mind, hear the piano accompaniment in your imagination. Repeat the process at least three times before moving onto the next line.

- Try repeating the phrase in your head instead of aloud. Rehearsing silently is a valuable method: not only does it help the memorisation process but it also saves wear and tear on the larynx.

- Use devices to link and recall key words or sections. For example, if the end of one line of a song is the word 'rove' and the next line begins with 'Or at…', you could link this sequence in your memory with the car make 'Rover'. Picture the car, remember its colour, the sound it makes and how soft the seats are as you sing the link between the two phrases. When approaching the end of the first phrase in a performance, a simple inner picture of the car will trigger the link into the next phrase. Or you could invent a mobile rodent called a 'rovorat'. The sillier images are often the most memorable. Things are more likely to become embedded in our memories if we have an emotional connection with them.

- Have an overview of the structure of a song; use this as a framework within which to place the detail of individual phrases. The structure can be the overall story in the text, or it can be the number of verses, or it can be the musical form. Preferably it is all of these. The overview can be a visual representation of the structure, or it can be a summary of the key points in the story.

- Vary the order in which you memorise the phrases. Don't always start at the beginning of a song or section of music. Try to work with short sections more than long ones. Divide the 'memorising music' part of your practice time into several short chunks rather than one long one.

- Learn the words and the melody simultaneously. It may not be helpful to try deconstructing a song into melody and words in order to memorise it. It has been shown that if the two are learnt simultaneously, they act as cues for each other [51].

- Even if you think that you have a song memorised well, do go back to the written score, or to the original recording, every now and then. You may have learnt and reinforced a mistake.

Chapter 6 Summary

Individual lesson structure:

- The initial conversation is a useful way to establish the pupil's vocal and emotional health.
- A good singing lesson will:
  - follow a basic structure: warm-up, exercises, repertoire
  - include sight-reading, theory and aural training: these can be integrated into the other elements of the lesson most of the time
  - integrate the body, mind and voice: physical embodiment of the singing process linked with imagination, understanding and communication
  - present one or at most two new ideas on which to work: communicate this clearly to the pupil so that they know how to practise it
  - send the pupil away in better voice than at the start (the speaking voice will be clearer and brighter) and in a more positive frame of mind. Pupils have to know that singing (and this includes practice at home) will make them feel better in themselves.
- Physical and emotional empathy is a useful way to understand your pupil's singing:
  - be careful not to pick up on unnecessary tension
  - remember to show good body use by example.
  - Use of touch in lessons can be valuable if it is managed sensibly.
  - Audio or video recordings of lessons is very helpful.

Athletes' training principles applied to singing:

- Know which muscles are already warmed-up (some of the postural muscles, also those used in speech).
- Be aware of those that need to be started 'from cold'.
- Training must be specific to the current repertoire.
- In order to increase stamina, the system can be overloaded (within reason).
- Train progressively by gradually increasing the workload.
- Balance hard and easy training.
- Vary the training.
- Train regularly.
- Rest effectively, resting the voice by engaging with another activity is better than just passive resting.

A suggested order for warming-up:

- **Set up your mind** – focus, no distractions.
- **Wake up the body** – running, dancing, brisk walk, run up stairs, arm circling.
- **Align your body** – posture work, Alexander Technique.
- **Specific flexibility exercises**, allowing muscles to lengthen – breathing, vocal glides.
- **Small and gentle movements leading on to extended movements** – e.g. small glides – large glides – multiple large glides, slow scales – fast scales, small pitch range – large pitch range, quiet singing – louder singing.
- **Varied and progressive exercises throughout.**

Personal practice:

- Effective practice is essential if progress is to be made.
- Practice must be regular, systematic and structured.
- Goals should be clear from the outset.
- Know when to stop: shorter more frequent practice sessions will be more effective.

Memorisation:

- Songs performed from memory will be sung with a deeper understanding and communicated more effectively.
- Memorising is time-consuming and can be frustrating for everyone.
- Give memorising your full attention, involve all your senses at the same time.
- Use varied strategies: aural, kinaesthetic and visual memories work better when linked with each other in the imagination.
- Memorise only short sections of a song at a time.
- Repeat the section at least three times, both out loud and in your head, before moving on.
- Have an overview of the song: this can be the different verses, the overall story or the harmonic structure. The overview can be a visual 'map' in your head.
- Vary the order in which you memorise sections of music: don't always start at the beginning.

Interlude F

Child protection issues

It is the responsibility of the teacher to ensure that the child feels safe at all times. The child must be protected from any situation which may result in physical or psychological damage.

It is also the teacher's responsibility to ensure that he does not place himself in a situation where a child might misinterpret information or gestures, leading to upset for the child or even an unfounded allegation against the teacher.

Singing inevitably triggers emotional responses, both from the implicit feelings in the text and music, and also because of the physically engaging nature of singing itself. If a teacher is working on an individual basis with a pupil, the relationship will be closer than that of a classroom teacher. The singing teacher will often find pupils will speak to them about issues that may be troubling them. Most of the time these will be everyday stories about friends, siblings, homework or other teachers. While it is important to hear and empathise with what the child has to say, it is not the role of the singing teacher to try to resolve the child's problems.

Occasionally, the child may disclose information of a more serious nature. The teacher cannot promise the child complete confidentiality; anything disclosed to the teacher has to be passed on to a higher authority if it concerns any type of abuse. There are different types of abuse: physical, emotional, sexual or neglect. Cases often involve more than one of these. If a child makes a disclosure, the teacher should remain calm, listen without interrogating and reassure the child that she is doing the right thing by telling someone. The teacher should then explain what has to be done next, make a note of what the child has said (after the event, not with the child in the room) and only tell people who absolutely need to know. If there is any possibility that you think a child is being abused, there should be a designated person to report this to. This may be the head of pastoral care in the child's school, or it may be necessary to report straight to the Social Services. Remember – it is not the responsibility of the teacher to decide whether or not the child is telling the truth.

It is also possible that you as the teacher may be implicated in an allegation. There are many ways to help prevent this from arising. If you are teaching in a school or music centre there should always be a glass panel in the door so that the lesson can potentially be observed by any passerby. Make sure that you and the child can be seen through the panel. Some schools and authorities ask that there should be absolutely no physical contact with a pupil. This makes teaching singing very difficult. If you are touching the pupil in order to assess muscular tension or in order to communicate a postural alignment, it can be done with the minimum of ambiguity. If you are touching a potentially sensitive area (belly, lower back, ribs), put the pupil's hand on his body with yours on top – that way you are only touching the back of the pupil's hand and yet you can still feel what is going on. Touching the shoulder, upper back, back of the neck or the head may be done directly. Touching the lips, front of the neck, lower abdomen or obviously personal areas is not acceptable. If you are touching the pupil, make sure that this is only done when it is directly related to the teaching process; never confuse it with an affectionate gesture. This professional detachment is important even with a pupil with whom you feel very familiar, for example a family member. The pupil needs to know what is work and what is social interaction. It is often possible to have more than one pupil in the room when the teacher wants to do some hands-on work. If the teacher is working in her own or the pupil's home, it is generally advisable to ask a parent to sit in on the lesson.

It is very helpful to make an audio recording of each lesson, with the permission of the pupil and his parents. Not only is this an accurate record of the interaction which has taken place, it is primarily an invaluable resource for practice.

Remember that child protection is ensuring your own safety as well as the child's. Keep everything absolutely open, direct and transparent and there will be little opportunity for ambiguity or misunderstanding.

Chapter 7

Vocal health and ill health

7.1 Why good voice use is important

The voice is our primary communication tool: the quality or timbre of our voice is like a mirror that reflects our health, age and mood. However, we tend to take it for granted unless it goes wrong. Voice problems affect both singing and spoken voice and so reduce our ability to communicate. We all at some time suffer from ill health that affects our voice: this may be just the common cold, or it may be longer-term voice loss. The cause of voice loss can be the way we use our voices, our lifestyle or as an indirect result of anxiety levels. These factors may or may not be within our direct control, but it may help if we can identify any causes.

It is also very important to remove any sense of guilt or blame. Anyone with a voice problem is unlikely to have caused it in a conscious and deliberate fashion. The disorder will be the result of a series of unfortunate situations, often outside the direct control of the individual. It is important to reassure the young singer that they are not alone, and that all voice problems can be helped if not removed altogether.

This section on vocal health, although specifically aimed at the needs of young singers, has much that can be applied to adult voice use.

Voice problems in children

Voice disorders are surprisingly common among school-age children. Up to 20% of children have what could be clinically defined as voice disorders [52, 53], although most of these cases are never referred for clinical treatment. Generally, these voices improve as the child grows and their voice use and function develops. However, if a child has a voice problem, it will affect many aspects of life. They will be less able to project their voice socially, in class, in sports or in singing/acting. This can have a negative impact on self-esteem and could have a greater effect on overall development.

Specific voice problems are described later in this chapter. If children have voice problems, poor singing technique is rarely the only cause. The voice problem is nearly always a result of over-use or misuse elsewhere: this may be in sports or in unsupervised singing. A common factor in most cases of voice disorder is high levels of anxiety in the child. Whatever the cause, the first casualty will be the child's singing. This is because singing requires the voice to use higher pitches and more precise vocal qualities than speech. It is crucial to help children to establish good habits of voice use when speaking, singing or shouting. It is of limited use to give a child good singing technique if this is not applied when shouting on the football field! Good vocal habits include voice use, voice awareness, related vocal health and general physical and emotional well-being.

Prevention of voice problems

We can learn about voice use from many disciplines: speech and language pathology, medicine, science, singing and acting. We can also look further at sports science and medicine for examples of good practice. Learning good voice use will result in awareness, and the management, of unnecessary tension in both speaking and singing voices, and also lessen the impact on the vocal folds. This awareness can help to anticipate and prevent voice loss.

Stress on the voice is measured as **vocal loading**. This is a measurement of the amount of impact the vocal fold tissues have to endure. Rapid or prolonged collision affects the structure of the cells within the vocal folds. Vocal loading is increased by three main factors:

- Amount of use: the number of hours you are speaking or singing relates directly to the number of vocal fold collisions in a day.
- Level of use: louder voicing requires the vocal folds to collide harder (think of the difference between clapping your hands quietly or loudly, then clap them loudly for a minute and see if they feel sore or hot).

- Emotional stress, which is often less easy to identify or deal with. Anxiety creates tension in the voice; it is therefore less efficient and prone to greater loading.

As well as these internal aspects there are external factors to consider such as room acoustics or pollution levels.

If a child develops a voice problem, it is useful to know that the cause is rarely one single factor; it will be a combination of several factors, all of which contribute to voice use, often with anxiety or stress as the final straw. Become aware of how you and your pupils use your voices, both speaking and singing. Try to identify good and bad situations or environments for teaching. Always warm up your own voice as well as the pupil's. These considerations can help you to have long and healthy years of speaking and singing.

Problem: the need to raise vocal volume

Children may have to speak in large rooms: even in the most disciplined classroom environment, there will always be a low level of background noise. In social situations, there may be a high level of background noise from television, music or other people speaking. School dining halls are often one of the noisiest places in which to try to have a conversation. Speaking or shouting in the open-air can also be problematic: the voice does not carry so effectively over distances, or there may be increased background noise, for example from traffic.

Solution

Using amplification is not a sign of failure – it is good common sense. It has been shown that the use of amplification is more effective at reducing vocal fatigue in teachers than using vocal hygiene methods [54]. If you only have to raise your voice occasionally, using good vocal technique for this is crucial. You can also use cupped hands to create a simple megaphone effect. The use of amplification can be a real help for children performing in poor acoustic conditions.

Problem: not enough variety in voice use

Children can fall into the habit of using a higher-impact voice quality than is necessary. Prolonged use of a hard tone not only reduces the effectiveness of communication, but it also tires the voice.

Solution

Explore different voice styles for different situations. First, try to establish the child's own neutral voice quality, then experiment with voices suitable for different situations: private chat, speaking on the phone or calling out during sport. When singing, try to aim for the singer never to sing at maximum power. Even for very loud passages, 90% is enough.

Problem: voice use while under emotional stress

If the speaker is under emotional stress, the muscles of the larynx are not working as efficiently, and the voice user is more prone to fatigue or injury. This single factor is the most common cause for children who suffer from voice disorders.

Solution

There are many ways to reduce stress levels; an easy one is to focus on your breathing. Pages 83–85 describe the action of low belly breathing. Breathing out tends to favour the **parasympathetic** (everyday bodily function) nervous system and breathing in is linked with the **sympathetic** (fight/flight) nervous system. Try breathing out for a count of eight and in for two or three; keep moving the breath throughout, don't hold your breath at all. If you consciously breathe out for twice to three times as long as you breathe in, you will help to redress the balance between these two systems. Controlled breathing can reduce the heart rate and calm you down – no wonder people find that singing makes them feel good.

Problem: speaking or vocalising during physical exercise

Physical exertion tends to rely on constricting the throat. This is not the time to use the voice (see **laryngeal constriction** pp. 94–96).

Solution

Save the vocal noises until after you have done the lifting or reaching for something. This is important during sport: try to encourage the child to stand still for the shouting and then to keep silent during the running or jumping or kicking or catching.

Problem: exposure to irritants

Some teaching rooms may have high levels of dust. Some people are more sensitive than others to particles or pollutants in the atmosphere.

Solution

If the singer is sensitive to dust or pollen levels, he may use an asthma inhaler. If dust levels are bothering you, the teacher, they are likely to be bothering others also and probably need to be dealt with. If children suffer from allergies they can benefit from having an ionizing air filter in the room. This will remove small particles from the air.

Problem: poor acoustic conditions

Classrooms, school halls and even music practice rooms have seldom been designed with acoustic properties in mind. If a room or hall has large, hard surfaces (walls, ceiling, floor), these will reflect sound around the space and increase the overall noise levels. The worst acoustic environment for this is an indoor swimming pool. Reflective surfaces are good for performances with a silent audience, but not good for teaching or rehearsing where there will always be some background noise. However, some sound reflection is useful. It can be very difficult to sing in a room that has a dull acoustic, the singer will tend to overwork the voice. Voices will be very hard to project in open-air spaces such as the playground or sports field.

<u>Solution</u>

If you are in a boomy room, curtains, rugs, pictures, books, corkboards, soft furnishings or screens will help to absorb or dissipate sound. If you are in a room with a dull acoustic, you can help by placing you or the singer facing a wall to reflect the sound back to him.

Pacing the voice

We know that the amount of voice use can contribute to vocal loading. Recent research has shown that vocal loading is reduced if the voice use is split into small units [55]. During a lesson, the singer will have periods of singing and periods of listening to the teacher. The same applies to singers in a choir. Try to increase the frequency at which you have short periods of voice rest in the lesson or rehearsal.

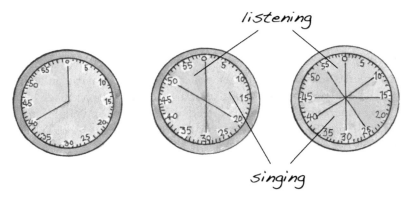

Figure 7.1: Try to increase the number of periods of rest in the lesson.

7.2 Lifestyle issues affecting vocal health for all singers: teachers and pupils

Eating and drinking

First, it may help to clarify exactly what happens to anything we swallow. As food or drink is passed back over the tongue and into the throat, the larynx lifts up and forward, the epiglottis shuts tightly over the top of it and the food/drink passes from the back of the mouth, down into the oesophagus and into the stomach. Nothing we swallow goes anywhere near the vocal folds; if it did, we would cough immediately. This means that water, lozenges, warm infusions or anything else that we may take to soothe the voice, are actually going straight into the stomach, bypassing the larynx altogether.

The **benefits of swallowing** are threefold. First, the action itself tends to shift any mucus sitting around on the vocal folds. Frequent swallowing can reduce coughing, clear thick phlegm and lubricate the vocal folds with their own supplies of thinner mucus. Second, sucking a lozenge may have a pleasant placebo effect: this is not to be undervalued. Third, any liquid swallowed will have a rehydrating effect on the whole body.

It is important to keep the body hydrated.

It is important to **keep the body hydrated**. If the throat is dry, or the cells of the vocal folds themselves are under-hydrated, then they will be more susceptible to injury. The little-and-often rule is a good one; try to keep a bottle of water on the go through the day. Children's lack of access to water in schools, or their reluctance to drink it, can be an issue to be aware of. The best way to know if your body is hydrated is from the colour of your urine. The advice is to 'pee pale'. If you drink more water than you need, it will only make you pee more frequently; it will have no further benefit.

Caffeine drinks (tea and especially coffee) can dehydrate, so try to balance a caffeine shot by following it with the equivalent quantity of water. **Alcohol** can also have a dehydrating effect the next day. Some singers like to have a small alcoholic drink before performing: this is not recommended for a number of reasons: it impairs muscle coordination and this impacts on pitching, rapid movement, quiet singing, articulation of text, breathing control and postural balance. Mental concentration and focus are reduced, memory is affected and self-perception is impaired. Even a small amount of alcohol will have a negative effect – if you can't drink and drive, you can't drink and sing to the best of your ability.

An alcoholic drink before performing is not recommended.

Sweetened fizzy drinks, milky drinks, chocolate, yoghurt and so on may encourage temporary mucus production in the throat for some people. If this is the case, avoid them immediately before and during singing. Their effect will wear off after about half an hour. Any build-up of mucus for longer than this is likely to have another cause.

Throat pastilles and lozenges have a very limited application. Ones that have a dehydrating or numbing effect are best to avoid before or during singing. Others work merely as a placebo, or at best they encourage frequent swallowing. Don't over-value them: sipping water is cheaper and just as effective.

Try not to eat just before going to bed. Eating a large meal late at night can encourage gastric reflux that can 'burn' the lining of the throat. Try to allow at least two hours after a meal before going to sleep.

Cigarette smoke deposits tar and other irritants directly on the vocal folds and in the respiratory system. At best this reduces efficiency, at worst husky voices and long-term illness. Cannabis smoke has an even worse effect on the tissues of the larynx than tobacco smoke.

Medications

All effective medications will have some sort of side effect. Sometimes this can involve drying of mucus membranes. This can be a potential problem for the singer as the voice may sound hoarse, and dry vocal folds may be more prone to injury. If in doubt, weigh up the importance of the medication with the importance of the performance. Consult your doctor before coming off any prescribed medication.

- Antihistamines can have a drying effect: check with the pharmacist.
- Asthma inhaler – it is important to use a spacer. This ensures that the larger (and ineffective) particles don't get into the respiratory tract. Some combined treatments of corticosteroid and bronchiodilator therapies can result in changes to the laryngeal mucosa – do check with your medical consultant.
- Some steroid decongestant nasal sprays can result in throat irritation and dryness.
- Decongestants used for longer than five days can cause problems as the membranes adjust to the medication. The rebound effect can result in a greater degree of congestion than before the medication was taken.
- Cough medicines: avoid ones that contain codeine (drying effect) or antihistamines. Expectorant medicines containing Guaifenesin can have a beneficial effect on the voice as they help to keep the vocal fold mucus thin and fluid. If the cough is caused by a dry atmosphere, asthma or gastric reflux, then cough medicine won't work.
- Antidepressants can have a drying effect.
- Oral contraceptives will either have no effect or a beneficial one. They may reduce premenstrual oedema of the vocal folds.
- One side effect of high-dosage Vitamin C supplements can be vocal dryness.

Excessive coughing or throat clearing may be habitual or it may be symptomatic of other issues such as rhinitis or reflux. Coughing or throat clearing is a forceful action of the vocal folds; when you feel the need to cough, try sipping a little water.

7.3 What to do when the voice goes wrong

Voice first aid

1 **Rest your voice** – If you feel you're losing your voice, or sounding husky, the first thing to do is to try to keep quiet. Avoid noisy environments and cancel social engagements (unless it's going to the theatre/ cinema).

2 **Steam** – Fill a bowl with boiling water, put your head over it with a towel over your head and breathe slowly until the water isn't steamy any more. It is best not to put anything in the water. Although menthol products can give the sensation of clearing the nose, all they are doing is over-sensitising the membranes and causing irritation.

3 **Sleep** – Losing your voice is not only inconvenient, it can also be very stressful. A few early nights may be all you need to get back on track. Sleep is essential for repair work on the tissues.

If the voice doesn't get better in two to three weeks, you may need a referral to a voice clinic; this is normally done through the family doctor.

7.4 Voice disorders in children

Organic voice disorders (not related to voice use)

- **Inflammation** is common but temporary. The symptoms can range from a croaky or breathy voice to complete voice loss; the cause can be viral, bacterial, allergy, reflux or over-use. Other inflammations such as pharyngitis, tonsillitis, sinusitis and rhinitis will not directly affect the action of the vocal folds unless there is considerable post-nasal drip.
- **Allergies** are common and generally need ongoing treatment. The symptoms can be hoarseness as well as nose blowing and sneezing. Common allergens include pollen, mould spores, dust, foods or cigarette smoke.
- **Gastroesophageal reflux** (stomach acid travelling up the oesophagus when you are lying down) is common and can cause throat inflammation and hoarseness. Treatment may include antacids to neutralise the pH, and/or raising the bed head.
- **Cysts** are fluid-filled dilated mucosal ducts; what causes them is unclear. Symptoms may be hoarseness or coughing. Treatment is surgical removal with accompanying speech therapy.

Functional voice disorders (related to voice use)

- **Polyps** are associated with healing after vocal trauma. Treatment is surgical removal with accompanying speech therapy.
- **Nodules** occur more frequently in boys than girls, but in more women than men. They are associated with high vocal loading over a prolonged period, often exacerbated by stress or anxiety. A nodule is a mass of fibrous tissue, similar to callouses. Treatment is usually voice therapy in the first instance.
- **Foreign objects** that block the airway have to be dealt with as an emergency. Smaller objects that become lodged in the throat (such as pieces of apple or carrot) can result in a coughing spasm, which may not dislodge the object. Inflammation develops with increasing vocal dysphonia. The inhalation of small objects such as pins, bits of glass, eggshells or parts of toys can result in vocal fold scarring or damage to the muscles or ligaments of the larynx.

- **Caustic ingestion** can either be ingestion of caustic fluids, passing through the pharynx, or inhalation of powder such as dishwasher powder. Site and severity depends on the amount and type of substance.
- **Psychological dysphonia** is surprisingly common. The larynx on examination will appear normal; coughing will have the associated phonatory response but the speaking voice will appear dysfunctional. This tends to be stress-related and a detailed history will be necessary. Psychological therapy will often be the necessary treatment.
- **Trauma** caused by an external force. Emergency intubation of a premature baby can result in contusions, lacerations and dislocation of the arytenoid cartilages. The symptoms when speech later develops are breathy or hoarse voice. There is the possibility of trauma occurring as a result of a direct blow to the neck, for example in a serious road traffic accident or sporting injury. Fracture of the larynx is less likely in children as their laryngeal cartilages are more flexible.

Contextual or environmental factors

- **Physical**. Acoustic environments with a high level of background noise will cause the child to speak loudly or shout for prolonged periods of time. These may include a noisy playground, school dining hall, swimming pool, sports stadium or even an unsupervised or poorly supervised classroom.
- **Social**. This element includes status and hierarchy and the use of appropriate levels of voicing, both in amount and loudness. Hours spent per day in large groups and a family history of voice problems are significant factors in incidence of dysphonia.
- **Temporal**. The time of day, stage of the school year or the child's past history of behaviour will all affect voice use.
- **Psychological factors**. Personality type would appear to be the single most influential factor on the occurrence of voice disorders in children. Several studies have suggested that the occurrence of nodules is more prevalent in children with anxiety symptoms. These children may present with either aggressive personalities or unnecessarily withdrawn, repressed personalities. Children who have unattainable goals (academic, musical or sporting), either as a result of parental pressure or sibling rivalry, are more likely to develop nodules.

Acoustic environments with a high level of background noise will cause the child to speak loudly...

Why intensive training sometimes goes wrong

As there is so little information on child singers, we have to look for some clues in the research on child athletes and adult singers. Performers will always strive to achieve more than their predecessors. With every individual there is a tipping point at which the level of performance becomes detrimental to health [56]. This point is often only discovered when the individual over-steps it. An Olympic athlete or a professional dancer may expect to suffer from some form of injury on occasion. However, any training for children should try to avoid this at all times. Children who perform to a high level, whether they are gymnasts, violinists or swimmers, despite a high degree of enthusiasm and commitment, are not consenting adults. They have often been persuaded into such activities by their parents or teachers and there is a moral obligation for all adults concerned to provide a duty of care to ensure that they do not suffer physical injury or emotional trauma as a direct result of their training.

Professional adult musicians

There has been much research in the field of performing arts medicine, some of which addresses the issues affecting professional adult singers. Many injuries experienced by professional musicians are related to repeated activity (repetitive strain injuries). In singers, the causes are often less easy to pinpoint, due to the physically internal situation of the mechanical parts involved in vocalising. There is, however, plenty of well-documented research into the vocal health of professional adult singers [57].

When looking at other health areas relevant to musicians, it has been suggested that, considering factors such as environmental noise, musicians are perhaps not as unhealthy as they should be. Orchestral musicians have to rehearse and perform in environments that often exceed Control of Noise at Work UK Government Regulations. Musicians have been shown to have a significant bilateral notch in their audiogram at 6kHz, suggesting the presence of noise-induced hearing loss [58]. We know from other available data just how much exposure to noise is needed in order to cause this level of hearing loss. Surprisingly, in professional musicians the levels of hearing loss are not as great as would be expected. It is possible that musicians are able to control or regulate the effect of the noise levels: if they know that, for example, a loud chord is imminent, it is possible subconsciously to reduce the impact on the auditory mechanism [58].

Orchestral musicians often rehearse in environments that exceed noise regulations.

Children who are trained to sing at a professional level

This possibility of intuitive self-regulation is a key finding of my own research into the vocal health of boy cathedral choristers [59]. We can see from this information that there may be risks associated with training children at a high level in any physical activity. Professional child singers fall into two broad categories: those in musical theatre productions and those in professional cathedral choirs. The factors contributing to vocal loading which I considered were the number of hours of singing per week, the proportion of performance hours within this time, the public profile of these performances, the vocal intensity (overall loudness) required, the level of expectation of achievement in other musical and academic activities and whether the children were at boarding or day school. When looking at all of these factors, the group who presented with the highest level of vocal recruitment and potential fatigue was boy cathedral choristers in central London.

I assessed their voices over a three-year period, and made comparisons with other similar groups of boys. For the basic evaluation of vocal health, I used a panel of experienced speech and language therapists to assess the quality of their speaking voices. The speaking voice will show evidence of fatigue, inflammation or inefficiency, the causes of which are many (see **voice disorders** p. 160). If the boys had been over-using or mis-using their singing voices, the evidence would be noticeable in their speaking voices. The surprising result was that the boys with the most demands on their voices turned out to have the healthiest voices. This could have been as a result of training or athletic conditioning. It could have been as a result of intuitive self-regulation, as with the orchestral musicians described in the previous section. As a singing teacher, I would like to think that it was as a result of education, persistent and regular reminders, but it is more likely that the boys only modify their behaviour if there is a tangible pay-off for them. It would take only a few occasions on which they have missed an opportunity as a result of over-use of their voice for them to learn to self-regulate. This of course applies to all of their voice use, especially in sport and social contexts.

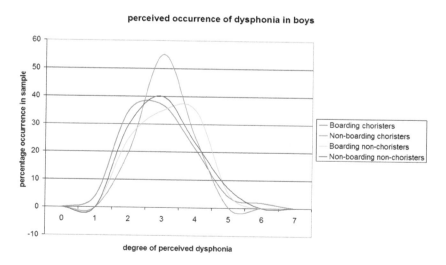

Figure 7.2: The perceived occurrence of dysphonia in boys, comparing the groups who were boarding and non-boarding at school, and those who were choristers and non-choristers.

From informal discussions with the boys, it is evident that they are consciously aware of their voice use in the choral environment and make adjustments accordingly. A senior boy may give a strong lead at the start of a musical phrase in order to give confidence to the younger boys; he may then ease off vocally once the phrase is underway. In sport and social contexts it is much less likely that the boys will be consciously regulating their voice use. Listening to them in the playground would suggest that they are free and uninhibited with their voice use. The evidence from the research would suggest, however, that caution is being exercised at some level, conscious or subconscious, at all times.

This is an interesting observation but not altogether surprising: a similar caution can be observed when one is watching young pianists and string players from a specialist music school when they are playing sport. They instinctively protect their hands from impact or strain. This care may have been drilled into them, but they never get carried away; they never go beyond safe limits. The healthy functioning of their hands means more to them than anything else. Any sport is much less tactile as a result of their self-regulatory care.

7.5 Performance expectations, anxieties and catastrophe theory

Stage fright or performance anxiety occurs at some level for every performer. Some young children seem less affected than others. Often the level of fear increases with emotional maturity of the individual, or the increased level of pressure associated with the performance.

The basic 'fight or flight' response is well documented, as so much of our general state of health depends on our ability to manage anxiety in our everyday lives. For the performer, many of the physiological reactions – sweating, shaking or hyperventilation – will have a negative effect on the performance outcome. As well as physiological reactions, the performer may have cognitive symptoms: these include fear of making mistakes, or feelings of inadequacy. The third component is behavioural: these symptoms result in the inability to perform tasks that are normally unproblematic.

Many singers perform better with some level of anxiety. This is known as adaptive anxiety in which the level of concentration and focus is enhanced. Levels of anxiety tend to be related to levels of confidence.

Stagefright!

If a singer has practised enough and mastered the task, the presence of an audience will enhance the level of performance. If the singer is under-prepared, the presence of an audience will inhibit task performance. In successive performances, anxiety can be both the cause and effect of failure. Nervous singers may sing badly because they have had negative experiences of performing in the past.

There is a crucial point in each individual beyond which the outcome can be disastrous. If physiological arousal (a measure of the heart rate of the individual) and cognitive anxiety (the degree of anxiety relating to performance expectation of the individual) increase to a critical level, then performance levels will rapidly deteriorate [56, 60]. Figure 7.3 illustrates the interaction of three variables: physiological arousal, cognitive anxiety and performance (the level at which the individual is able to perform) at any single point in time. Catastrophe theory suggests that once this critical level of cognitive anxiety is exceeded, it is not possible to regain performance levels with small adjustments to the predictor variables, physiological arousal and cognitive anxiety. This is illustrated by the sudden dip and further collapse of the performance level as the cognitive anxiety increases. If cognitive anxiety is kept to a low level, then physiological arousal and performance level can have a positive correlation.

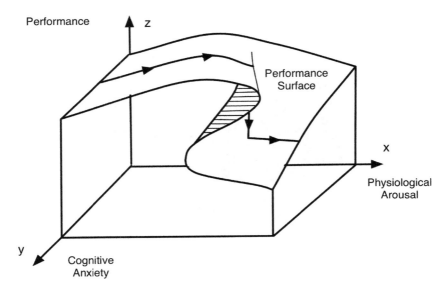

Figure 7.3: Catastrophe model of performance [56].

This work comes from the field of sports and sporting achievement. As we have found elsewhere, there is a strong similarity between sport and singing; they both rely on the systematic training of a specific group of muscles to perform a complicated task at an expert attainment level. Performance anxiety can have a detrimental effect on any performance, whether that is music, dance or sports [11, 61, 62].

Strategies for anxiety management

Problem-focused strategies will deal directly with the actual situation. Emotion-focused strategies will deal with the way the performer perceives the situation. The most important thing is to rehearse and practise to a level at which the task can be automatic. This is especially important when singing from memory. It can help if the singer has the chance to 'try out' performances on imagined or small audiences. An audience of fellow-performers can be extremely supportive and encouraging. Some relaxation techniques can be useful: a simple one is using controlled breathing as preparation for performance (see p. 152). This works on the theory that the in-breath stimulates the nervous system (fight or flight) and the out-breath stimulates the sympathetic nervous system (general, everyday metabolic activities).

Stress-buster exercise

Place your hands on your belly to ensure that you are breathing low in the body. Breathe out most of the air in your lungs. Breathe in to a count of 3 (counting at the rate of seconds can help to tie in with the natural heart rate) and out to a count of 6. After two or three cycles, increase the out-breath to a count of 8. Maintain this until you feel still and focused. This can often result in a lowering of the heart rate as well as an overall sense of calm.

If performance anxieties are an ongoing and serious problem, it may be advisable to seek the advice of an expert therapist. Therapies that have been shown to be useful include cognitive-behavioural therapy, systematic desensitisation, behaviour modification, psychodynamic therapy, hypnotherapy, or body-centred methods such as Alexander technique, yoga, t'ai chi or massage.

'When you perform, it's the most important thing in the world to you and at the same time it's not important at all; people are not going to die, the world isn't going to stop turning.' Joanna MacGregor, pianist.

7.6 Golden rules for healthy voice use

- Water is the best drink for singers. Have a drink of water as soon as you wake up in the morning and keep a bottle on the go during the day.
- Warm-up before using your voice: this applies to speaking as well as singing.
- If you are ill or tired, you will not be using your voice as efficiently; stop if you feel strained.
- If you have a voice problem or just a tired voice, the best immediate help is steam from boiled water alone.

- Be aware of how you use your voice at all times, not just when you are singing.
- You are more likely to get ill or use your voice less effectively if you are stressed or worried: chill out!
- Sleep is the best cure for many problems.

Chapter 7 Summary

- We take vocal health for granted until it goes wrong.
- Voice disorders are surprisingly common in children.
- Vocal problems are rarely due to a single cause, they normally arise from a combination of factors.
- Singing habits are rarely the cause but the problem may be most apparent when singing.
- A voice problem is generally nobody's fault. Reassure the singer and remove any sense of guilt or blame.
- Prevention is better than cure.
- Effective prevention requires awareness of voice use at all times.

Vocal loading, or impact on the voice, is increased by:

- Amount of use (number of minutes or hours per day).
- Level of use (loudness).
- Emotional stress (affecting muscle function).

Strategies for good voice use:

- Coping with emotional stress, use breathing strategies such as counting for longer when you breathe out than when you breathe in.
- Avoid using the voice while exerting the body.
- Be aware of dust and pollen levels.
- Try to dampen boomy acoustics and use reflectors in dry acoustics.
- Pace the voice – take frequent voice rests.
- Keep swallowing, this disperses excess mucus and lubricates the vocal folds.
- Use amplification if necessary or use hands as a megaphone.
- Avoid speaking in noisy environments.

- Explore different voice qualities, establish a more gentle neutral voice.
- Avoid excess coughing or throat clearing.

Eating and drinking:

- Keep hydrated by drinking enough water.
- Caffeine and alcohol will dehydrate the body.
- Dairy products may cause temporary mucus production; this will disperse in 20–30 minutes.
- Lozenges are mainly useful as a placebo.
- Avoid eating late at night.
- Be aware of any medications which may cause dehydration or irritation of the larynx.

Voice disorders:

- Voice disorders can be organic (not related to voice use) or functional (related to voice use).
- The most common factor in the causes of voice disorders is high anxiety levels.

Performance anxiety or stage fright:

- Stage fright is a natural physical response to fear.
- A controlled level of anxiety will enhance performance.
- If the level of physiological arousal (e.g. heart-rate) and the level of cognitive anxiety are both beyond a certain level, the result is a catastrophic reduction in performance outcome.
- Focusing attention on breathing patterns can help to reduce anxiety.
- A confident performance is more likely if you are well-prepared.

If the voice goes wrong:

- Rest.
- Steam.
- Sleep.
- If problems persist for more than three weeks, visit a doctor.

Drink water

°c

Warm up

Don't sing when
ill or tired

Steam helps

Be aware
of your voice

Don't
stress

Sleep well

Figure 7.4: Keeping your voice healthy.

Interlude G

Choral singing

Singing in a group or a choir is the most important musical experience a young singer can have. It is common, but unfortunately not universal, in all Western education to have classroom songs as an integral part of early schooling. For many children, this opportunity remains throughout their school years. As was illustrated in Chapter 2, singing in choirs has been shown to have benefits for health and well-being throughout life. At a basic level, any group singing activity is positive, whether it is in a religious context or as part of the crowd at a sporting event. If it is presented as part of the education of children, the experience is almost entirely dependent on the skill and expertise of the choral leader or conductor. This is an impossibly difficult task, as it requires an individual who is not only an expert in vocal pedagogy, but also a skilled conductor and an inspirational communicator. Again, I am hoping that I can provide some help with the first of these three attributes. This section is not intended as information on how to conduct a choir, but is to give an indication of some issues that may arise from asking a group of individuals to sing 'as one'.

It may be tempting to offer instruction to the group that has a technical language. The problem with using technical language or imagery is that it is essentially a code, which may be understood differently by different individuals. If you are a singing teacher who can coach each of the choir members individually as well as in the group, then you may be able to use specific terminology and be understood in the same way by each singer. If any of the singers have lessons with another teacher, or don't have lessons at all, then there is the possibility for misunderstanding. Examples of images that are relatively easy to understand:

- **bright,**
- **warm,**
- **ringing or**
- **dark.**

More problematic examples could be:

- **Clear** – clear of what? Of breathiness? Of vibrato? Of creak?
- **Open** – open where? Open mouth, soft palate, upper pharynx or lower pharynx? Does this actually mean bright? Or simple/naive?

- **Rich** – dark? Or warm? Or with vibrato?
- **Full** – loud? Or warm? Or warm and bright?

Then there are examples of images that sound like technical instructions:

- **'on the breath'** – does this mean breathy tone? Or light? It's difficult to sing without breath!
- **'covered'** – does this mean a modified vowel in the upper range? Or a lower larynx?
- **'supported'** – does this mean sustained to the end of the phrase? Or richer tone? Or louder?
- **'focused'** – this could mean bright and ringing, or it could mean non-breathy.

Even if it is understood what voice quality is required, none of these terms contains any clue as to how this could be achieved.

It can be easier to interpret directions if they are unvocal emotional triggers such as, **'secretly excited', 'tentative', 'to a sleeping baby'** or **'exuberant'**. If in doubt, it may be most helpful for the singer to ask the conductor what sort of mood they are trying to convey, rather than what sort of vocal technique they are wanting. A mood will communicate to everyone, whereas technical language is a potential minefield.

There are several persistent ideas in choral training that are distinctly unhelpful for individual singers. The problem here is that the conductor may be listening for the overall effect on the group sound. This may seem to be enhanced by certain instructions or images. Unfortunately, this sound may be at the expense of the individual. Here we are returning to the idea presented at the very start of the book. Many methods used by choral conductors and singing teachers have evolved from intelligent guesswork. People will devise theories based on the evidence available, if they aren't aware of a full-enough picture, the methods may be flawed.

- *Sing with a 'yawning' sensation to open the throat.* This is a short cut to a fuller, richer sound with potentially disastrous consequences for the singer. The reason why it has been recommended in the past is that it appears to open the throat. This widening and lengthening could be thought to make the voice bigger and fuller. In fact, nearly all of the actions will cause a problem. First, it will stretch the pharynx, inhibiting any mobility in the tongue and soft palate: this will limit clear articulation of text. It will also depress the tongue, pressing it down onto the top of the larynx. The larynx is mobile and this downward movement will make the vocal tract longer. The effect of this is to increase the low frequencies in the sound, making the voice sound richer – that's why conductors like the sound. Unfortunately, this is not the best way to lower the larynx as it will inhibit its flexibility, especially the ability to sing high pitches easily. The result can often be a hooty sound that is flat. Try yawning and speaking at the same time – it's not a beautiful or flexible sound!

- *Sing as if you have a hot potato on your tongue.* This has a similar effect to the yawn. The habits created by these actions can take years to unlearn.
- *Smile when singing to lift the sound* (or, even worse, to *'lift' the cheekbones* – I'm yet to meet a singer whose skull has independently moving parts). We need to differentiate between a natural smile, coming from a genuinely happy emotion, and an artificial grin. The grimace will effectively shorten the vocal tract as the sides of the lips are pulled back. This shortening of the vocal tract will remove lower frequencies in the sound and create an impression that the pitch is sharper. In reality, the effect is merely to limit the resonant properties of the sound and to create unnecessary tension in the singer. Try singing a simple held note, maybe an open [a] vowel, relax the face then do a big cheesy smile, the smile brings noticeable tension to the voice. A small smile, if it is a genuine feeling, will not cause any problems unless you are singing a sad song.
- *Open your mouth wide to make a better sound.* There is a difference between allowing the jaw to drop, and opening the mouth wide as if taking a bite out of an apple. Allowing the jaw to drop will enable the tongue to work effectively, and will provide the necessary resonant space for singing. Opening the mouth wide necessitates the forward movement of the jaw, which will pull on the back wall of the pharynx and the soft palate. Opening the end of a flute or clarinet won't necessarily make a better sound. Also, any action that creates more tension in the singer has to be questioned. Dropping the jaw is beneficial, pulling it down or forward induces tension and is counter-productive.

If there is any doubt about instructions given, do ask the teacher or conductor to explain what they are doing and why. It is good for children to learn how to question their teachers and leaders. A curious but polite query presented in a non-confrontational manner in a quiet moment should be given the time and respect it needs.

Singers who spend a lot of their time sight-reading music are keen to enhance how they hear their voice in order to monitor their tuning and accuracy. One way in which to do this is to pull the tongue back in the throat. This effectively blocks the sound, containing it within the throat and boosting the internal hearing directly through the bone and into the ear. The sound to the singer can be richer as bones conduct more low-frequency sounds. The problems arising are firstly that the singer develops habits of tongue root tension with all the longer-term consequences (p. 106–7). Another problem can arise from the misrepresentation of frequencies in the sound. Tuning is perceptual and is dependent on the balance of formants within the sound (p. 119–123). If this is distorted because too much of the auditory feedback is through the bone, the singer will not be able to tell if they are in tune or not.

Even with a conductor who is giving helpful and creative advice, there may be other habits arising from choral singing. The conductor's body language is crucial. There is much more known about this now and conductors who study and train will be made aware of this. For example, gestures for the in-breath made at waist level will encourage lower breathing than those made at chest level. A sudden and unprepared upbeat will encourage a quick and tense in-breath on the upbeat and an even an ensuing nod on the downbeat. Remember that the singers will mirror every action of the conductor's body. They will also mirror the way that the voice is used in speaking as well as singing.

Another factor to consider is the positioning of the singers. In some choirs, especially some church choirs, the singers are grouped on two sides of the space, facing each other. The conductor is usually at one end of the line of singers, requiring them all to turn to face him or her. This would be possible, except that the singers are often sharing copies of the music. This is an important way in which the younger singers are shown how to follow the written music by the older singers. Unfortunately it means that half of the singers will be looking at music on one side of their body and a conductor on the other side of their body. This will result in a turned head for singing. If this asymmetrical position is maintained for any length of time, it will result in the muscles on one side of the larynx becoming more developed than those on the other. This can be observed in ex-cathedral choristers who can be seen to have a deviated larynx, pulling to one side as it rises [63]. This problem is easily overcome by moving the singers around within the choir.

Other issues arising from choral singing may come about as the individual attempts either to blend with or to lead the singers around them. Blending with less experienced or younger singers can often compromise the vocal production of the singer. This can inhibit their development if the habit persists. Attempts to lead a section usually result in vocal fatigue. These issues are not limited to young singers; they can apply to all who sing in choirs.

It is possible that we will never find a satisfactory answer to the never-ending question of whether solo singers can also sing in choirs. The singer may feel that their vocal individuality is always at some level of compromise in order to blend with the group. If we are asking young singers to manipulate their sound to fit in with the conductor's overall perception of the sound, surely they will need the flexibility resulting from an even more advanced technique. We know that this is unlikely in the school/university age group. If we also consider the personal expressiveness of a singer, how does this fit into a choral mould? I suspect that for most singers, there isn't an answer: the musical and social reward of choral singing will be greater than the individually expressive needs of the solo singer. If the singer can manage to balance both activities, she will be all the richer for it.

Philip

Philip is an experienced professional tenor in his early 30s. His case is high-lighted here just to illustrate how the choral compromise can be an issue, even for the most experienced singer. Philip spends about two thirds of his working year with choral ensembles: he sings with most of the top professional groups in the UK. The rest of his singing work is opera and oratorio solo singing. When he has a singing lesson following a tour with a choir, we always have to spend time working on regaining the projection in the upper part of his range. This is subtly and subconsciously reduced as he instinctively blends his sound with his fellow-singers. Although we have discussed this and he knows it is happening, he still needs help to make the transition. Once his ringing tone is restored, my ears hurt and I know we've hit the spot for solo singing!

Chapter 8

Children with specific
individual needs

'There is a growing body of evidence showing that music can play an important role in the education of children with learning difficulties. Its repetitive, regular and therefore predictable structures could have been (and maybe originally were) purpose-made for young minds in the early stages of perceptual and cognitive development – craving order in a complex and confusing world. For teachers, therapists and carers, though, music has much more to offer than pleasing patterns in sound. It can lend its simple, symmetrical shapes to language, reining in the apparently wilful diversity of verbal communication. It can act as an auditory frame for reference for movement – setting the pace for action, and serving as a metaphor for reaching high and stooping low. It can scaffold social encounters – giving children the confidence to embark on that most tricky business of reaching out into the capricious world of other people. Above all, the sheer pleasure of music can permeate any other area of experience and learning which it touches, boosting interest and helping to sustain concentration.' Adam Ockelford, Professor of Music, University of Roehampton, [64]

In any group of children within mainstream education, there will be a percentage whose educational or health profile requires greater understanding of the requirements and abilities of the child. This chapter will not aim to guide teachers working within specialist schools, but it will describe many of the issues that may arise within mainstream education. Most adult individuals feel that they have adapted to the limitations of their mind or body. These may be perceived as wide-ranging, from having a poor memory to having short arms. If individuals have any kind of deficit in dealing with the world around them, then they adopt strategies to compensate. In many ways, the politically correct terminology of 'differently abled' shows that each individual is just that – an individual person with an individual way of understanding and relating to the rest of the word. It can be frustrating to be labelled for what you can't do, rather than known for what you can do.

Children who have been identified with a specific educational need have generally been given these labels in order to help them, rather than to define them by their limitations. They are eligible for extra assistance in school and their needs can often be summarised according to a particular, recognised condition. With this in mind, teachers can equip themselves with as much knowledge as possible from a generalised model, and then apply this carefully and appropriately to the individual. All schools have a designated special needs coordinator as well as having extra staff within the classroom to give help to individual children with recognised needs. Each child to whom this applies will have her own individual education plan, identifying the teaching approach best for them. It is useful to establish links with the schoolteacher and the parent in order to establish the most positive approach that the singing teacher can take. Most importantly – ask the child what things he finds helpful.

Terminology used to describe these children ranges from 'special needs', '… impairment' and 'disabled' through to 'learning difficulties' or 'behavioural difficulties'. To group all of these children together under one umbrella term is at best challenging and at worst totally unhelpful. There is a big divide between those children who have lost something, for example had a severe injury and lost the use of their legs, or lost their sight or hearing, and those who were born with their condition. There is also a divide between children who can't do something and children who won't do something. The ones who 'won't' will find changes difficult, frustrating or upsetting, but with the right guidance, they may be able to make developments. Don't try to change aspects of the ones who can't change.

Almost all of these issues are found in varying degrees in each individual. Degrees of Asperger's syndrome or dyslexia can often go unnoticed; the person concerned will have enough strategies to compensate almost entirely. At the other end of the spectrum, severe degrees of a condition such as autism can result in the person spending an entire life in full-time specialist care. The education department within the English government currently defines the groups in the following areas: the recommended code of practice is that each child is to be treated as an individual and have personalised learning. The singing teacher may come across a pupil with any one, or indeed a combination, of these issues.

Communication and interaction:

- speech and language delay, impairments, disorders
- specific learning difficulties, e.g. dyslexia and dyspraxia
- hearing impairment
- autistic spectrum
- moderate, severe, profound learning difficulties.

Cognition and learning:

- moderate, severe or profound learning difficulties
- specific learning difficulties, such as dyslexia or dyspraxia
- physical and sensory impairments
- autistic spectrum
- behavioural difficulties.

Sensory and physical needs:

- profound and permanent deafness or visual impairment
- lesser levels of hearing or visual loss
- physical impairments
- neurological difficulties
- metabolic difficulties
- emotional stress
- physical fatigue.

Behavioural, emotional and social needs:

- withdrawn or isolated
- disruptive and disturbing
- hyperactive and lacking concentration
- immature social skills
- challenging behaviours arising from other complex special needs.

Some general guidance for the teacher

Baseline assessment

It is important to do a detailed musical assessment when you start to teach any child. Make a note of what the child *can* do: this enables you to work from his strengths. It is also worth bearing in mind that children with difficulties may make slower progress. This can be frustrating for both teacher and pupil. If you have made a baseline assessment, it is encouraging to look back and see what has actually been achieved – you may be surprised.

Encouragement and confidence

Pupils who see that their progress is different from their peers may become frustrated. They may be too frightened of failure even to have a go at something. Positive and believable feedback is essential throughout the teaching process.

Where possible, keep a dialogue with the pupil. Ask, is this working? Is this approach helpful? Is this how you'd like it? Can you think of another way to work around this?

Multi-sensory learning

Kinaesthetic methods, those where the pupil will use movement or touch, are beneficial for all music teaching. When learning a rhythm, use clapping and stamping – stamp the beat and clap the rhythm over this. The stamping uses each side of the body in turn, which will help with all aspects of learning and coordination. Initially just try clapping one beat to each stamp and then two beats per stamp. Gradually increase the complexity, lesson by lesson. Begin each time with revising the basics and then introduce only one new rhythm per lesson.

In order to learn musical concepts such as legato/staccato, encourage the pupil to embody these by doing the actions: for legato they can stroke their arm, for staccato they can poke a finger into the palm of their hand, for example. Encourage the pupil to use hand gestures to indicate high and low pitch or phrase length, or when learning to release the abdominal muscles in order to allow a low and easy in-breath. With imaginative teaching a song can become a dance – the links between the two are inseparable throughout the world.

Emphasis on working directly in sound, for example call and response work, can reduce the amount of learning using written materials. Kodály methods use hand signals (visual and kinaesthetic) linked to pitches and durations (aural). Some pupils may remember key ideas, words or emotions if they are linked to textures such as sandpaper, fur, silk or foil.

Short-term memory

Give small chunks of information, only one idea at a time. Allow time for this to become assimilated before introducing more. Use visual and imaginative metaphors to trigger the memory. Have a clear learning structure that you share with the pupil.

Long-term memory

Repetition is the key. At the start of the lesson, revise the main points covered in the last lesson, repeat them until the pupil is comfortable and then move on. At the end of the lesson, summarise the new information.

Avoiding distractions

Peripheral noise may be more distracting to the pupil, as may visual distractions such as posters, clutter in the room or what may be seen through windows. Be aware of the pupil's field of vision when positioning them in the room. Distractions are not just aural or visual; the child may be sensitive to smells such as perfume, air freshener or food. Unnecessary information on the printed page may also be distracting: pupils can sometimes become dizzy during writing or reading.

Noise may distract the pupil, as may visual distractions.

Clear practice structure

Give the pupil a specific plan for practice: the order in which things should be done, what to do and how to do it. Encourage the pupil to learn songs by listening to recordings. If you can use a recording of a voice type that is similar to the pupil's own, this is very helpful.

Reading music

Music is a complicated system of symbols. Time signatures look like fractions but are not: short horizontal lines have a different meaning from curved ones or vertical ones. Try to keep the initial learning mainly aural and kinaesthetic. It may help the pupil if notation is introduced after she has learnt the song. It can help if the notation given to the child is as simple as possible; remove all unnecessary instructions from the score. Make copies in larger print. Shiny white paper can be more difficult to read from, so copy music onto coloured paper – a different colour for each song.

When sight-reading, the sheer amount of information on the page can be baffling. You can limit this by giving the child another piece of plain paper with a window cut out of it to lay over the music. As you move the window over the printed page, only a small amount of information can be seen at any one time. As the pupil becomes more familiar with reading music, they can be encouraged to read ahead. This means that they are looking at what is to come, rather than what is currently being sung. Reading pitches and rhythms simultaneously may be too complicated and daunting: try doing them one at a time.

8.1 Dyslexia, dyscalculia and dyspraxia

Dyslexia is a disorder relating to literacy skills, dyscalculia relates to number skills and dyspraxia is a developmental coordination disorder. They are all genetic conditions and cannot be 'cured' as such. There may be an overlap between them and other related conditions. It is possible that the problems encountered by these pupils are due to an underlying abnormal neurological timing or temporal processing. This temporal processing can be improved through training, and music is one obvious way to achieve this. 'Musicality' does not seem to be negatively affected by these conditions; the problem is with the tools of music – the physical coordination, the written notation, the complex timing skills and the learning and memory work involved. Knowing how to engage with the child and which strategies can help you in your teaching can enable the child to achieve success through music in ways which may not be possible elsewhere.

Up to 10% of the population may have some form of dyslexia. There are many definitions of the condition; in essence it is when the individual has literacy skills below what one would expect from their level of cognitive ability. It tends to be noticed in children with above-average IQ. Dyslexia affects the area of the brain that deals with language, leading to differences in the way in which information is processed and affecting the underlying skills needed for learning to read, write and spell. Because it involves problems with sequencing, if a list of instructions is given, the short-term memory will not cope. It can also affect the transfer from short into long-term memory. Poor short-term memory can lead to other problems such as disorganisation, lack of concentration, anxiety and low self-esteem.

Dyscalculia is a condition that affects the ability to acquire arithmetical skills. It has been referred to as number dyslexia. Dyscalculic pupils may have difficulty understanding simple number concepts: they may have problems telling the time or dealing with money. Even if they produce a correct answer or use a correct method, they may do so mechanically and without confidence or understanding. They will have problems with following sequential directions and organising detailed information.

Dyspraxia is an impairment of the organisation of movement. It is associated with problems of perception, language and thought and can often occur along with dyslexia. Boys are four times more likely to be affected than girls. Other names for dyspraxia include developmental coordination disorder (DCD), perceptuo-motor dysfunction and motor learning difficulties. It used to be known as clumsy child syndrome. Children with this disorder have difficulty in processing the visuospatial information needed to guide their motor actions. They may not be able to recall or plan complex motor activities such as dancing, catching or throwing a ball with accuracy, or producing fluent, legible handwriting. There can be a history of early delay in the development of motor skills such as sitting up, crawling or walking. Often, these children are described as clumsy or forgetful.

Individuals with dyslexia or dyscalculia will have developed compensatory processes in order to survive in the world around them. They may have a much more developed sense of the whole picture. They may be specifically skilled in having a concept in their mind of a whole piece of music. They may have a much more highly developed sense of kinaesthetic or auditory awareness. They may have excellent listening skills. Because of the issues affecting physical coordination, the musical dyspraxic child may well be able to find more immediate musical pleasure from singing than from playing an instrument.

8.2 Autism and Asperger's syndrome

Current thinking is that autism has a genetic cause. Whilst every individual with autism will have different issues, there are some common areas to consider. Classic autism and Asperger's syndrome have some links. Children with either condition will have social communication issues and narrow interests often linked to repetitive actions. The differences between them are in language development and IQ. Autistic children have delayed language skills and an IQ anywhere on the scale; Asperger's children have no specific language problems, may be of above-average intelligence and often tend to be high-functioning intellectually. Both conditions are more common in boys than in girls. The shared issue is one of a lack of empathy: the child finds it difficult or impossible to understand how another person can perceive the world. He does not understand feelings or emotions in the same way as other children.

The autistic child dislikes anything unexpected: surprises or changes of plan can be extremely distressing for them. Conversely, they will derive comfort and security from repeating simple actions, sometimes for hours at a time.

Children with either autism or Asperger's syndrome may well excel at music. Music is a system; printed music is a generally unambiguous set of instructions. Learning to play an instrument involves daily repetition of tasks and exercises. The child may find real comfort in this. Some highly successful concert pianists would come under the diagnosis of autism or Asperger's. Many autistic children are more sensitive to sounds and music: they often have perfect pitch and may be more highly aware of the upper partials or qualities of the sound. Some individuals may develop more advanced musical skills than might be expected, while a few may be prodigiously talented.

The therapeutic value of musical training for the child on the autistic spectrum is as important as for the child with dyslexia. Music can have the power to stimulate emotions and intensify our social experience. This may be partly due to the activity of mirror neurons within the brain. These will automatically respond to physical and emotional stimuli, giving us a type of parallel experience. As individuals with autism may have less well-developed mirror neuron systems, engaging with music may be an ideal way to help develop and reinforce emotional experience.

Singing is an additional challenge as it involves text and the direct expression of emotion. If these issues are addressed effectively, learning to sing can be a positively helpful way to engage, explore and expand the experience of an autistic child.

Some helpful approaches for the teacher with pupils on the autistic spectrum

It is most important that all communication is simple, direct and unambiguous.

Mark (Asperger's syndrome, age 8)

Mark had joined us for a Sunday morning bike ride along the river, just so that his parents could have a bit of a break. He was a good cyclist where there were no traffic considerations. After a while, we stopped and I got out a picnic for everyone. As I handed round bottles of water, Mark looked put out, 'I haven't got anything.'

'It's ok,' I said, 'Here's your water.'

He shot an indignant look at me, 'That's not mine.'

Of course it wasn't his: he'd never even seen it before. How could I make such an obvious mistake? No amount of explanation or reasoning could persuade him otherwise. He wouldn't even try the biscuits I'd brought. From that moment on, not only was I stupid and not to be trusted, but the whole of his morning had been ruined by me.

Had I said 'Here is some water; I brought it along for you to drink,' the morning might have had a different outcome.

Explain everything you are going to do in a clear sequence, for example: 'Here is where you stand. I am going to give you some exercises for your singing. I will help you with each one as we go. You will then sing through your song from last week and we can do some work to improve it. We will then have a look through a new song. When the lesson has finished you can go back to your classroom. Does that all sound like a good plan?' A younger autistic child may find it easier to understand if you draw a picture of each event as you explain it in a sequence. It is important that she feels secure in a predictable environment. When the structure is in place, the child may feel happier to direct the progress and content of the lesson herself.

Allow the child to process information and work out each step before applying it or moving on. If you interrupt the child's thinking, you may have to return to the start. Children with Asperger's syndrome will often have a high-functioning intellect; they will respect you as an expert in your subject, as detail is important to them. With them, you don't have to keep language simple but it must be unambiguous. Non-literal language such as metaphor, irony, humour, figurative language and sarcasm is to be avoided. The apparent ease and knowledge of the pupil can be misleading for the teacher.

When preparing pupils for a performance or a music exam, take them through the whole procedure including walking on and off stage and acknowledging applause. Let them see the performance space and try it out beforehand.

8.3 ADD or ADHD

Attention deficit hyperactivity disorder (ADHD) is the most common childhood-onset behavioural disorder, typically diagnosed at age 5 or 6. The three key symptoms are hyperactivity, impulsivity and inattention. Those affected have a greatly reduced ability to maintain attention without being distracted, to control what they're doing or saying and to control the amount of physical activity appropriate to the situation. ADHD is also called attention deficit disorder (ADD) or hyperactivity. The disorder shouldn't be confused with normal, boisterous childhood behaviour.

Pupils with ADHD can become exclusively focused on a task if it interests them, this can often be music – either listening to music or practising an instrument. This focus can become an obsession with perfectionism. Although the process itself can be frustrating, the attention to detail and relentless repetition can have a great outcome for a pupil's technical skills on a musical instrument.

Some helpful approaches for the teacher with a pupil with ADHD

First, avoid any distractions either in or outside the room (see p. 182). Ensure that you have the attention of the pupil before giving an instruction. Encourage the pupil to verbalise tasks and instruction – first to the teacher and then silently to himself. Use frequent eye contact. Include a greater variety of activities within the lesson.

Focus on short-term steps rather than long-term plans. Agree on the structure of the lesson at the start, and summarise the work achieved at the end. Give the pupil a specific plan for practice: the order in which things should be done, what to do and how to do it.

8.4 Asthmatics

Asthma is an allergic response to environmental triggers such as dust, animal hair, pollen or smoke. The nerve endings in the airways are more sensitive and so become easily irritated. This causes the air passages of the lungs to become inflamed. The muscles in the smaller airways can also be triggered to contract. In an asthma attack, this inflammation and/or muscular contraction causes the airways to narrow making it difficult to get air in and out of the lungs.

Guidelines for teachers of an asthmatic pupil

The most obvious sign of the asthmatic child is wheezing on inhalation, although many asthmatics have intermittent symptoms and may go for weeks without any problems. It is important to establish whether noisy inhalation is due to asthma and not laryngeal constriction. The asthmatic singer may find it more difficult to sustain long phrases. Generally speaking, if the asthmatic singer learns effective breathing technique for singing, this can be useful for them in their everyday life. Many professional singers who are asthmatic will claim that their symptoms would be far worse had they not had singing training.

It is important to ensure that the asthmatic child has her inhaler with her at all times. If a child has an asthma attack, in an emergency any inhaler is better than no inhaler.

8.5 Eczema

This condition will not directly affect singing ability, although it can be distracting for the pupil. If a child has bad eczema he will find that a hot, dry room exacerbates his symptoms. If a child is scratching continuously, especially a young child, it can help to give him something to hold. This can be something with tactile interest such as a smooth object, a shell or a wooden shape. He may find that squeezing and shaping a ball of blu-

189

tack provides enough distraction from the itching to be able to focus on singing.

8.6 Fatigue-related conditions

This includes illnesses such as glandular fever, ME (myalgic encephal-opathy), chronic fatigue syndrome and post-viral fatigue syndrome. Although there are common factors with all of these illnesses, they can present in an individual-specific way. It is best to discuss with the pupil what she feels she can or can't do. It is important to allow the pupil to direct the pace of lessons: pushing her or stretching her will not help.

8.7 Hearing impairment

'Hearing' is not just a function of our ears. We feel vibrations throughout our body and these can be identified as specific pitches and timbres, if the listener is trained. A child with hearing impairment may be far more acutely tuned-in to these kinaesthetic interpretations of sound. Spoken word is more difficult to feel in the body and children who have been deaf from birth have to be trained to speak. They often have a more backed tongue position as they try to feel their own voices: this can identify them as sounding 'different'. It is also worth remembering that it is rare for a deaf child to have absolutely no hearing at all. The child's residual hearing may not be sufficient to enable them to understand speech, but may be sufficient to appreciate music. Some recent research by Dean Shibita at the University of Washington suggests that the auditory cortex in deaf people becomes linked to their processing of physical vibrations. This may mean that they 'hear' music in the same way as those with normal hearing.

The occurrence of hearing loss in schoolchildren is not often well documented. Many children are not diagnosed until they are older. Hearing loss can be temporary, such as glue-ear, where the eustachian tube becomes blocked (usually due to an infection) and the middle ear becomes filled with a sticky substance. Although this is temporary, it can have important implications for children who either miss out on key information in their education, or withdraw from social contact. Hearing loss probably affects about 6% of schoolchildren at some time.

Some helpful approaches for the teacher of children with hearing impairment

Deaf children can be taught to sing, and they can be taught to sing in tune. They find pitch discrimination easier in the lower frequencies and consequently their vocal range may be limited to the lower part of their voice. Group singing can help.

Multi-sensory approaches are vital. Use visual stimuli such as hand gestures, linked with vibratory ones such as feeling the teacher's larynx, face or head, the audio speakers or the piano.

Rhythmic patterns may be easier to establish than pitches: link visual clues with auditory ones.

8.8 Visual impairment

Nearly all blind and partially sighted children will be in mainstream education. They will all have a designated teacher or assistant to help them. Visually impaired, and especially totally blind, pupils may have physical and proprioceptive issues. They often develop a habit of walking with the head slightly back (to avoid painful collisions); this alignment will have implications for singing. They will, however, be very used to physical contact from the teacher as a means of communicating physical ideas; in fact it will become an essential learning method for them. Remember to warn a blind person that you are about to touch her. If teaching through touch presents any difficulties, it is fine to ask for a parent or another pupil to be present in the room in order to avoid ambiguities or misunderstandings.

Modified Staff Notation is a less cluttered layout of music, in which instructions are located in easier places; the print is large and clear. Ensure that the pupil has glasses that are the correct focal length for reading music; this may not be the same distance from the eyes as for reading books.

Braille music is available for pupils who can already read braille, although the differences between braille and printed music need to be understood. This information on braille is from the RNIB website:

'Scanning for a particular sign is much harder in braille music than in print. In braille music, all the signs have to appear left to right, one at a time. This is different from stave notation, where notes are displayed vertically in chords, and other *signs like phrase markings are put above or below them. Related to this is the issue of space: a bar of Braille music can take up considerably more room than in print notation. Reading and following scores can therefore be challenging, as there may be just one bar per page. Although braille music can represent all the commonly used signs in conventional stave notation, braille music uses fewer signs than print music and they are frequently used in combination. This means that it's easy for new readers of braille to get confused. For brevity, braille music uses repeat signs more frequently than in print. Braille also needs to use a sign to specify in which octave to play a particular note.'*

Specific eye conditions: tracking problems such as nystagmus

This affects between 1 in 1000 and 1 in 2000 individuals. The eyes may not appear to look in the same direction, or there may be uncontrolled movement of the eyes, usually from side to side, but sometimes the eyes swing up and down or even in a circular movement.

Many children with visual tracking issues do not have other health problems. Their vision may vary during the day as it is likely to be affected by emotional and physical factors such as stress, tiredness, nervousness or unfamiliar surroundings. They may tire more easily than other people because of the extra effort involved in looking at things. Some find a visual aid such as a magnifier helpful. Large print material should always be made available and extra time should be given for reading information.

Albinism

Albinism is a group of genetic conditions that causes a lack of pigment. It affects 1 in 15,000 of the population. It can affect only the eyes (ocular albinism) or both the eyes and skin (oculocutaneous albinism). Corrective lenses (i.e. glasses or contact lenses) and low vision aids (i.e. magnifiers or telescopes) can provide some clarification. Most people with albinism use their vision for reading, and do not use braille. Some have vision good enough to drive a car.

The individual child's vision can also vary somewhat based on the sunlight and artificial light in the classroom, fatigue and other factors that vary from hour to hour and day to day. If the pupil is used to rehearsing in one room, the transfer to performance space may be too bright for comfort.

8.9 Cerebral palsy

It is estimated that 1 in every 400 children is affected by cerebral palsy. Cerebral palsy is a term used to describe a group of chronic neurological conditions affecting body movements and muscle coordination. It is caused by damage to one or more specific areas of the brain, usually occurring during foetal development or infancy. It also can occur before, during or shortly following birth. Cerebral palsy is not a progressive condition, it will not get worse. However, the symptoms can put strain on the body, which may cause problems in later life.

There are several types of cerebral palsy. Children will suffer from stiffness or involuntary muscle movement. They may have problems relating to posture and general coordination, although the degree to which they are affected varies considerably. Intellectual ability is not normally affected. In general, the child should be able to learn to sing.

Standing for any length of time may be problematic: the pupil may prefer to hold onto something or to be seated. This should be carried through into performance.

In specific cases, children with athetoid or dyskinetic cerebral palsy may have problems with coordinating the mouth, tongue and larynx. This will affect singing significantly. Spastic quadriplegia is the most severe type of cerebral palsy, caused by extensive damage to the brain. Children with this will find speaking difficult, and may have moderate to severe learning difficulties.

8.10 Down's syndrome

This is a genetic condition where the child has an extra copy of a particular chromosome. It occurs in around 1 in 1000 births and it results in varying degrees of learning disability. A child with Down's syndrome has characteristic physical features: he will typically have a flat facial profile and eyes that slant upwards. Other facial features include smaller ears, a flat back of the head and protruding tongue. The child may have hearing or sight problems, and will be more susceptible to infections.

Singing can be enormously beneficial for the Down's syndrome child. It can help her to develop speech and language, to memorise information or new words through repetition of a song, and to interact with a group. It can help to develop motor coordination as well as to improve self-confidence.

8.11 Cystic fibrosis

Cystic fibrosis occurs in 1 in every 2500 people. It is a condition which mainly affects the lungs and pancreas, but can affect other parts of the body including the liver, nose and sinuses, reproductive organs and sweat glands. Normally cells in these parts of the body make mucus and other watery juices and secretions. In people with cystic fibrosis, these cells do not function correctly and make mucus and secretions which are thicker than normal. For the singer, the most significant ongoing issue concerns the thick mucus in the lungs. This can limit lung function and lead to a persistent cough. The pupil is also more likely to suffer from respiratory infections. A chronic illness such as cystic fibrosis may cause a delay in puberty. This will affect the development of the voice into the early 20s.

Some helpful approaches for the teacher of the pupil with cystic fibrosis

The pupil with cystic fibrosis must stay clear of respiratory tract infections. Try to avoid contact which may pass on infections such as touching hands or faces.

Assess the level of physical development of the pupil on appearance and not age, especially in the adolescent.

Have flexible expectations of goals and timescales; the pupil may have stays in hospital, which will disrupt progress.

The lungs may have scarring from repeated infections; the pupil may not have the lung capacity or stamina of a healthy individual.

Chapter 8 Summary

General guidance for inclusive teaching:

- Any group of children will have individuals with particular educational or physical needs.
- Labels applied to these children can be useful servants but poor masters.
- Try to establish links with the school teachers and parents, and discuss suitable methods of learning directly with the child.
- The issues discussed in the chapter can occur in varying degrees in each individual, they are often complex and multiple.
- Make a baseline assessment of every child.
- Give realistic encouragement and believable feedback.
- Encourage multi-sensory learning using kinaesthetic (physical feeling), aural and visual stimuli.
- Introduce new ideas incrementally.
- Avoid distractions in the room, either strong smells or visual clutter.
- Give a clear practice structure.
- Keep written music notation simple.

Interlude H

Historical outline of singing training for children

Ancient Greek vases
depicted singing lessons.

Greek vase paintings from the fourth century BC show teacher and pupil seated opposite each other, often with a lyre or kithara in their hands and the singing depicted as bubbles coming out of their mouths. Plato wrote that the purpose of teaching singing to children was in the importance of the text. It was a means by which they could learn tales of heroism and moral instruction.

In the Middle Ages in Europe, all formal musical education was within the church. Children have sung in the daily worship of cathedrals, abbeys or collegiate churches in Britain for 1400 years: the music-making of the church has followed a variable course with invasions, reformation, civil war and neglect [65]. This musical heritage itself arose from the Jewish practice of training Levite boys to sing psalms. Initially, boys were in training for the clergy, but they would sing in the daily worship. In

680, Bede writes of a choral workshop at Wearmouth, where an expert musician gave instruction to the cantors in the 'theory and practice of singing'. Incidentally, for the first few hundred years of Christianity in Britain, girls also sang. They were young girls who were to become nuns. The re-introduction of girls into singing in modern cathedral foundations from the 1990s was controversial at the time but can be seen to have ancient roots. Child oblation, the promising of a child to the church, would have been considered the highest honour for an Anglo-Saxon family. From the twelfth century, the practice of child oblation was dropped and boys were educated in cathedrals and collegiate churches where they were not necessarily bound for monastic life.

Between 1350 and 1550 there was a blossoming of church music with a huge expansion of the number of churches and chapels in which choristers sang. Monasteries re-introduced boys into their singing as lay-members. Adult (male) singers in the choirs were no longer ordained clergy but were employed primarily for their musical skills. Collegiate churches were established at Eton; Winchester; New College, Magdalen and Christ Church, Oxford; and King's College, Cambridge. The music itself was notated and complex: polyphony for five parts or more can be seen in the Old Hall Manuscript and in the Eton Choirbook. Unfortunately little music survives from this period as much was destroyed during the following reformation of religious practice in England. In the final years of Henry VIII's reign, composers such as Tallis, Sheppard and Tye produced some of their finest music for cathedral choirs.

Some contemporary accounts suggest that choristers could be rather disorderly: in Southwell in 1503 the choristers' robes were 'disgracefully torn' and the boys themselves were said to 'rave and swear'. There are numerous accounts of lay clerks and organists in the late sixteenth and early seventeenth century as drunkards, gamblers, blasphemers and fornicators. There were, however, centres of real excellence such as the Chapel Royal. Composers such as Purcell, Byrd, Mundy, Morley, Weelkes, Gibbons and Tomkins produced works that are still pivotal to cathedral music today. A side-line of some of the choristers in places such as Westminster, St Paul's and the Chapel Royal was participating in dramatic performances. Some of these were at court and others were in public theatres. In the 1570s the choristers of St Paul's Cathedral had their own raised stage, with seating for about a hundred people.

In Europe, children were given musical training in orphanages run by the church. These were known as *conservatori* and they became the training institutions responsible for producing the great operatic singers and composers of the eighteenth century. Initially these singers were male only and included the castrati singers who sang both on stage and in European churches. Later in the eighteenth and nineteenth century female singers were to come from these *conservatori*. The instruction received by the children was a highly organised system of musical exercises, designed to enable the understanding of musical structures and facilitate composition. The exercises were primarily sung by the children. There were many different schools of training and the material was passed on as an aural tradition, very few written sources survive. Composers such as Rossini and Puccini undertook this method of training from a young age [66].

With the Restoration of the English monarchy in 1660 following Cromwell, the fate of cathedral music and the boy chorister went into slow decline. Between 1700 and 1850 secular music in England thrived. Opera was popular, and music societies were as common as choral societies. Church music was, however, almost wholly abandoned by the highest profile composers of the time. Chorister numbers diminished: the boys suffered neglect and maltreatment in much the same way as other children at the time who were employed in the mines and factories. A report of a Sunday evensong at St Paul's Cathedral in 1871 stated that 'at no time did there appear to be more than an irregular confused hum of children's voices, trying to sing something of which the majority seemed incapable' [67].

Reform of the choristers' welfare was initiated by Maria Hackett in 1811 and continued by her until the 1870s. She was an educated lady with some financial means, enabling her to devote her life to improving the welfare of choristers. This resembled the work of Elizabeth Fry in the prisons and Florence Nightingale in nursing. By the middle of the century chorister numbers had begun to rise, and welfare standards had begun to improve.

In Paris, the Conservatoire National de Musique was established in 1795. This took children from as young as 8 years old to train as musicians. Regular classes in solfège were the foundation for their musical training: sight-singing was learnt before vocal or instrumental technique. This became the foundation for the teaching of Kodály in the early twentieth century.

From the late seventeenth century, private musical education of children in the middle and upper classes began to flourish [68]. It was assumed that infants had a naturally musical ear and that this could be trained from the age of 6 or 7. Musical notation was taught alongside the playing of an instrument. From the late eighteenth century we have some evidence of musical games; music education was addressed in a more playful manner. Musical literacy was taught along the same lines as the grammar of language. The approach was instructive rather than creative. Music lessons were rarely part of school education, and tended to be seen as an activity primarily for girls. Singing and instrumental ability were seen as attractive accomplishments for young ladies of this time. There are very few portrayals in art works of the time where boys are associated with any instrument other than those with military connections such as drums or bugles.

Throughout the nineteenth century, schooling became universal for all children and singing was a compulsory part of the curriculum. The manner by which this was taught varied but tended to use systems such as Tonic Sol-fa. Children learned musical notation and were often able to sight-sing in three or four parts by the time they finished their schooling. John Spencer Curwen (1847–1916) was president of the Tonic Sol-fa College from 1880 and was influential in British music education for many years. He made several tours of European countries, observing and recording the methods used for singing and music education. These were varied and included the fixed-doh system, where doh is always C. He saw in action the Chevé system of cypher notation, where the pitches of the scale are represented by numbers, with 1 as the keynote of a major key. He surmised that systematic learning of musical notation was crucial. He was critical of schools that relied on aural rote learning rather than reading.

Twentieth-century educational theory often based itself on the concept that 'ontogeny recapitulates phylogeny'. In other words, our physical and intellectual development from conception to adult in some way mirrors the evolution of the human species. This theory led to the progressive introduction of musical media in children's education. The early stages would begin with percussion, moving through dance, and progressing to singing. Many composers such as Carl Orff and Benjamin Britten wrote specifically for children. Wilfrid Mellers (*Musical Times* 1964) suggested that the only age group not represented by the music of contemporary classical composers was the teenager. For them, the most relevant music was, of course, pop and rock.

Postlude

Having read this book, you will, I hope be encouraged in your teaching practice to seek out further study of the subject. Research shows that teachers with qualifications, both those who have undergone teacher training and those who partake in continuing professional development schemes, all teach better on average than their untrained colleagues. The most effective learning environment for children is one staffed by highly qualified and motivated teachers, providing a context for children to play and share initiatives, and where pupils are encouraged to be part of the learning experience.

The very fact that you are reading a book on teaching suggests that you are open to learning and are prepared to try out new ideas. Have the courage to step outside your comfortable habitual methods and try some new repertoire, or use a new exercise.

It is also essential, as a teacher, to know one's limitations. Sometimes the relationship with a pupil just doesn't work out and it is important to recognise this and to be able to guide the pupil towards another, more suitable teacher. Also, no one can know everything. Your limitation may be a lack of knowledge of jazz improvisation, suitable operatic roles for a tenor in his early thirties, pop repertoire, fun songs for the under-5s or how to teach singers with basic pitch-matching problems. That is not a problem at all if you know where to refer the pupil to fill in any gaps. Give and take between teachers is far more common than it used to be, you don't need to 'possess' a pupil. Hopefully the pupil is coming to you voluntarily and can benefit from input from other teachers too.

As I said at the beginning, a book cannot tell you how to teach and a book cannot tell you how to sing. In order to try to present information rather than instruction, I have focused much of the text on the detailed mechanics of singing. Singing is a whole body-mind experience. It relies on imagination and instinct. A performance without inspiration is a poor experience for all concerned. Teaching likewise depends on intuition, empathy and imagination.

You don't need to
'possess' a student...

Educating people is of such importance, it must be seen as a serious undertaking. On the other hand, the process of teaching can be playful and creative. Remember that humans are curious and resourceful. Using the evidence you have, try things out, invent your own exercises. If they don't work, try again. If they do work, share them.

'The principal goal of education is to create individuals who are capable of doing new things, not simply of repeating what other generations have done — people who are creative, innovative and discoverers.' Jean Piaget

Glossary

Adduction	The closing action of the vocal folds. The opposite of abduction, or opening.
Adolescent	An adolescent is an individual aged from the onset of puberty to the age of about 18.
Adolescent voice change	The changes within the voice, in both boys and girls, that occur as a direct result of hormonal changes in the body during adolescence.
Arytenoid cartilage	Two cartilages located on the back of the **cricoid** cartilage, They have a rocking and tipping action; this is responsible for **vocal fold abduction** and **adduction**.
Belting	A term used in **CCM** singing. It describes a high-impact sound, similar to shouting or calling. It is used occasionally to achieve an exciting and emotionally charged sound.
Breathiness	The sound of air escaping through the **glottis**. This can be as a result of inefficient vocal fold **adduction**, generally due to an imbalance of muscular activity within the **larynx**.
Cambiata	A term used to categorise boys' voices during **adolescent voice change**. This is a useful term to use when their vocal pitch range doesn't fall into the adult classifications of alto, tenor, baritone or bass.
Cervical spine	The seven disc-like bones (**vertebrae**) at the top of the spine that form the vertical support for the head.

Child	A boy or girl from the age of 1 year to the onset of puberty.
Classical	Western Art Music from the renaissance to the present day.
Contemporary Commercial Music (CCM)	Musical theatre, pop, rock, gospel, folk, jazz and musical vernacular.
Creak	The vocal sound made at the lowest pitch possible. Creak quality can also overlay sound at higher pitches; in this case, it is caused by irregular vibrations of the vocal folds.
Cricoid cartilage	The ring-shaped cartilage in the lower part of the larynx. The vocal folds insert onto this on the inside at the back.
Cricothyroid	The muscle attached to the front sides of the thyroid cartilage and the outer sides of the cricoid cartilage. When contracted it pulls the thyroid forward and down, thereby lengthening the vocal folds and causing them to vibrate at a higher pitch.
Cross-training	A term used to describe the use of a variety of training activities; it comes from sports training.
Deep neck flexors	The muscles responsible for keeping the cervical vertebrae upright and relatively straight.
Diaphragm	The principal muscle of inspiration. It is dome-shaped and located inside the ribcage. Contraction results in a downward movement, pulling air into the lungs.
Dysphonia or voice disorders	Any vocal health problem resulting in poor or inefficient voice function.
Epiglottis	The flap of cartilage at the front of the larynx, which closes over the top during swallowing to prevent food entering the larynx.
Epilarynx	The space within the larynx, above the vocal folds and below the epiglottis and aryepiglottic membranes.

Expiration	The action of breathing out. The opposite of **inspiration**.
Falsetto	Method of voice production used to extend the vocal range higher by releasing the **thyroarytenoid** muscle, stiffening the **vocal ligament** and lengthening the **vocal folds**. It is characteristically breathy and hooty.
Fine motor skills	The coordination of small muscle movements; for example, those in the fingers or the **larynx**.
Formant	A relatively strong group of **harmonics**. A formant can be reinforced in a resonant cavity or space with the corresponding resonant **frequency**. In the voice, the first two formants define the vowel quality. Formants three, four and five define other aspects of vocal quality, mostly concerned with the projection of the voice.
Frequency	See **Pitch**.
Fundamental frequency	The lowest and generally strongest frequency within a frequency spectrum. It is the actual frequency of vibrations that are causing the sound. The other frequencies are **harmonics**.
Gasro-oesophagal reflux disorder (GORD), gastric reflux, acid reflux	If stomach acids enter the oesophagus (gullet), normally when lying down, they can irritate the **larynx**. This irritation can result in coughing, throat clearing or **dysphonia**. It can go unnoticed for some time, as the sufferer may not actually feel any discomfort. It is exacerbated in those who eat shortly before going to bed.
Glottis	The space between the **vocal folds**.
Gross motor skills	The coordination of large muscle movements; for example, running, ball skills or dancing.
Harmonics	The vibrations of the harmonic series. These are present in the sound spectrum of all vocal sounds. They occur as predetermined multiples of the fundamental frequency. These can be known as **overtones** or **upper partials**.

Hyoid	The horseshoe shaped bone at the top of the **larynx**.
Infant	A child under 1 year of age.
Inspiration	The action of breathing in. The opposite of **expiration**.
Intonation	The precise tuning of a note.
Kinaesthetic	A physical awareness, the sensation of feeling and doing.
Laryngeal constriction	The closing action of the **larynx** (see **Larynx**, primary function). If this response is triggered to a small degree during voicing, it will adversely affect the sound, causing it to become harsh and eventually to crack.
Larynx	The tube-like organ located at the top of the windpipe, containing the vocal folds. Its primary function is as a valve to stop anything other than air from entering the lungs. Its secondary function it to trap air in the lungs enabling the abdominal muscles to push when high exertion is required. Its third function is to make sound.
Loudness, amplitude, sound pressure level	Sound pressure level defines the amplitude of the sound energy, this is measured in decibels (dB) and is heard as loudness levels.
Motherese	The vocal sounds made by an adult as communication with an infant. These may be speaking, singing, cooing or babbling. They are generally of a sing-song nature and higher pitched than normal speech.
Motor memory	An instinctive muscular action related to a specific task, such as walking or speaking. The combination of muscle use will be encoded in the brain as a rehearsed neurological pathway.
Mucosal layer	The outer layer or layers of the **vocal folds** (and other surfaces within the body). A healthy and moist mucosal layer is essential for efficient voicing.

Mucosal wave	The ripple action that passes around the **vocal fold**, from bottom to top, as a consequence of the nature of the vocal fold collision. The degree of movement of the mucosal layer can generate energy in the upper **partials** of the sound spectrum.
Onset	The start of any sound. Glottal: voicing that starts with a small click, as in the exclamation 'Uh-oh!', and whose purpose is often emphasis of the following vowel. It is created by the vocal folds coming together before the exhaling airflow starts. Simultaneous: voicing that starts gently from nothing without any air escaping first. The vocal folds are brought together at the same time as the airflow starts. Aspirate: sound that starts with audible air escaping before the tone begins (e.g. 'ha'). Creak: sounds like a door creaking at the start of the sound. It's created by loose, irregular vibration of the vocal folds.
Overtones	See **Harmonics**.
Parasympathetic nervous system	Part of the autonomic nervous system, which controls functions outside our conscious direction. The parasympathetic division controls the 'everyday' functions of digestion, cell repair and respiration.
Pharyngeal constrictor	Muscles around the wall of the pharynx. When these contract, the throat is narrowed and the larynx is lifted. They are part of the swallowing mechanism.
Pharynx	The throat, or the tube-like space between the back of the mouth and the top of the **larynx**.
Phonemes	Units of spoken or sung sound that are the components of words.
Pitch or Fundamental frequency	Frequency is the number of vibrations per second in a sound, measured in Hertz (Hz) a higher pitch has a larger frequency. Middle C has a fundamental frequency of 261.6Hz (see **Harmonics**).

Posterior glottic chink	The gap at the back of the **vocal folds** observed when voicing. This is due to inefficient action of the muscles controlling the **arytenoid** cartilages. It is common in girls and women and results in a breathy tone.
Practice	The sequence of warming up the muscles of the voice, repeating technical exercises and rehearsing repertoire. This is a regular, private activity of any performer or student.
Psychomotor skill	An action, combination of or sequence of actions that has been rehearsed and memorised. An example is riding a bicycle. See **Muscle memory**.
Puberphonia	The use of a falsetto speaking voice during and after puberty. This can result from an underlying reluctance to accept the physical changes accompanying the process of puberty.
Repertoire	Music available to or known by the singer. This can be individual songs or choral music.
Roughness	A slight grating quality in the sound: irregular vibrations in the **vocal folds** result in intermittent vocal sounds in addition to the **fundamental frequency**.
Soft palate or velum	The soft tissue at the back of the roof of the mouth. When raised, it forms a seal between the mouth and the nasal cavity. During swallowing, this action prevents food from entering the nose.
Stamina	The ability to sustain extended activity without fatigue.
Strap muscles	Muscles able to lower the **larynx**. These are relatively weak and can only function effectively if the suspensory muscles are released.
Support	A term used to describe the action of maintaining breath activity suitable for singing. It can be ambiguous and is often misunderstood.

Sympathetic nervous system	Part of the autonomic nervous system, which controls functions outside our conscious direction. The sympathetic nervous system operates when the body is under threat or in a state of arousal. The responses include an increased heart rate and sweating, everyday functions such as digestion are inhibited.
Thyroarytenoid	The muscle within the vocal fold, along with the **vocalis**. It attaches to the **thyroid** cartilage at the front and the **arytenoid** cartilages at the back. When it contracts, it shortens the **vocal folds**, lowering the **frequency** of vocal fold vibration.
Thyroid cartilage	A laryngeal cartilage shaped like a curved shield. It can be felt at the front of the neck as the main prominent part of the **larynx**.
Tongue retraction	The action of pulling back the tongue in the mouth. This can result in vowel distortion.
Tongue root tension	The action of pressing the base of the tongue onto the **hyoid** bone. This can be felt as pressure by the fingers placed under the chin.
Twang, ring or the singers' formant	The sound quality generated by enhanced upper **partials** in the sound, in particular **formants** three, four and five, at around 3000Hz. Enhancing these is a particularly effective way to boost the projection of the voice. Human ears are acutely sensitive to these **frequencies**.
Vibrato	A periodic fluctuation of **pitch** and **loudness**, normally at about seven cycles per second. This can be a naturally occurring phenomenon and is linked to muscle tremor.
Vocal folds	The membranous tissues stretched horizontally across the **larynx**. They contribute to the valve function of the larynx. When brought together on **exhalation**, the edges vibrate in the airstream to make sound.

Vocal health	The state of health of the entire vocal system, but in particular, the **vocal folds** themselves.
Vocal ligament	Part of the **vocal folds**, this runs within the length of the membrane and contributes to the tensile strength of the vocal fold. It is not evident in **infants** but can be seen in the **adolescent** vocal fold.
Vocal loading	A measure of strain on the voice. Contributory factors include amount of voice use [69], level of voice use (loudness) and anxiety levels.
Vocal register	Different parts of the range of the human voice. Chest register has often been used to refer to the lower range, and is characterised by richness of sound. Head register has often been used to describe the upper vocal range, characterised by its lighter, simpler quality. The terms chest and head voice are historic terms that date from when it was thought that the sounds were produced in those different areas. We now know that this is inaccurate, and that sound is produced in the **larynx**.
Vocal timbre	The timbre or quality of the sound depends on the distribution and intensity of the upper partials or **harmonics** in the sound spectrum. Strong higher harmonics will result in a brighter sound, lower harmonics give a darker sound.
Vocal tract	The space between the vocal folds and the lips or nostrils. This comprises the **epilarynx**, **pharynx**, oral and nasal cavity.
Vocalis	The muscle within the vocal fold, along with the **thyroaryteniod**. It attaches to the **thyroid** cartilage at the front and the **arytenoid** cartilages at the back. When it contracts, it shortens the **vocal folds**, lowering the **frequency** of vocal fold vibration.
Vowel modification	The action of consciously altering the vowel in order to exploit the resonant properties of the **vocal tract** at particular pitches

Young adult   A young adult is from the age of about eighteen to the mid-twenties.

Phonetic symbols

These are universal symbols use to represent spoken or sung sounds. All text can be unambiguously represented by a phonetic transcription. In this book, the phonetic symbols used have been limited to just a few vowel sounds.

	UK English	US English	German	French	Italian
[i]	bead	bead	bieten	lis	chi
[I]	bid	bid	bitten	–	–
[e]	bed	–	beten	est	vero
[ɛ]	–	bed	betten	père	bene
[æ]	bad	bad	–	–	–
[a]	–	–	hatten	sa	bagno
[ə]	ago	ago	getan	demain	–
[ʊ]	put	good	Mutter	–	–
[ʌ]	up	bud	–	–	–
[ɑ]	part	pod	–	–	caro
[ɔ]	hot	–	Sonne	votre	possa
[o]	–	bode	Sohn	beaux	come
[u]	pool	booed	mut	ou	burro

Recommended further reading by subject area

Singing teaching

Bunch, M. (1997). *Dynamics of the Singing Voice*. Wien, New York, Springer-Verlag.

Callaghan, J. (2000). *Singing and Voice Science*. San Diego, Singular Publishing Group.

Chapman, J. (2006). *Singing and Teaching Singing*. San Diego, Plural Publishing.

Chipman, B. J. (2008). *Singing with Mind, Body and Soul*. Tuscon, Arizona. Wheatmark

Dayme, M. B. (2005). *The Performer's Voice*. New York, W Norton & company.

Doscher, B. (1994). *The Functional Unity of the Singing Voice*, Metuchen, N.J., Scarecrow Press.

Harrison, S., G. F. Welch, et al. eds. (2012). *Perspectives on Males and Singing*, New York, Springer.

Kayes, G. (2004). *Singing and the Actor*. London, A&C Black.

Miller, R. (1986). *The Structure of Singing*. New York, Schirmer Books.

Nair, G. (1999). *Voice - Tradition and Technology*. San Diego, Singular Publishing Group.

Potter, J., ed. (2000). *The Cambridge Companion to Singing*. Cambridge, Cambridge University Press.

Shewell, C. (2009). *Voice Work, Art and Science in Changing Voices*. Chichester, Wiley-Blackwell.

Vennard, W. (1967). *Singing: The Mechanism and the Technic*. New York, Carl Fischer.

Children's voices

Andrews, M. L. (2002). *Voice Treatment for Children and Adolescents*. San Diego, Singular Thomson Learning.

Cooksey, J. M. (1999). *Working with Adolescent Voices*. St Louis, Concordia.

Mould, A. (2007). *The English Chorister: A History*. London, Hambledon Continuum.

Phillips, K. H. (1996). *Teaching Kids to Sing*. Belmont, California, Schirmer.

Williams, J. (2012). Cathedral choirs in the United Kingdom: The professional boy chorister. In: *Perspectives on Males and Singing*. S. Harrison, G. F. Welch and A. Adler. London, Springer.

Wilson, D. K. (1979). *Voice Problems of Children*. Baltimore, Williams & Wilkins.

Music publications

Hill, B. and M. Stocks (2011). *Inside Music*. London, The Voices Foundation.

Hobbs, L. and V. Veysey Campbell, eds. (2012). *Changing Voices*. London, Peters Edition Ltd.

Any Voiceworks publications, Oxford University Press

Children's physical growth and sport science

Cram, S. (2001). *The Young Athlete's Handbook*. Champaign, Il, Human Kinetics.

Malina, R. M., C. Bouchard, et al. (2004). *Growth, Maturation and Physical Activity*. Champaign, Illinois, Human Kinetics.

Tanner, J. M. (1964). *Growth at Adolescence: With a General Consideration of the Effects of Hereditary and Environmental Factors upon Growth and Maturation from Birth to Maturity*. Oxford, Blackwell Scientific.

Voice function and anatomy

Hixon, T. J. (1987). *Respiratory Function in Speech and Song*. Boston, College-Hill Press.

Howard, D. and J. Angus (2001). *Acoustics and Psychoacoustics*. Oxford, Focal Press.

Mithen, S. (2006). *The Singing Neanderthals*. Cambridge, Mass., Harvard University Press.

Netter, F. H. (1997). *Atlas of Human Anatomy*. East Hannover, New Jersey, Novartis.

Sundberg, J. (1987). *The Science of the Singing Voice*. Dekalb, Illinois, Northern Illinois University Press.

Thurman, L. and G. Welch, eds. (2000). *Bodymind and Voice*. The VoiceCare Network.

Titze, I. R. (1994). *Principles of Voice Production*. Englewood Cliffs NJ, Prentice Hall.

Vocal health

Greene, M. and L. Mathieson (2001). *The Voice and its Disorders*. Philadelphia, Whurr.

Harris, T., S. Harris, et al. (1998). *The Voice Clinic Handbook*. London, Whurr.

Morrison, M. and L. Rammage (1994). *The Management of Voice Disorders.* London, Chapman and Hall Medical.

Sataloff, R. T. (1998). *Vocal Health and Pedagogy.* San Diego, Singular.

Watson, A. (2009). *The Biology of Musical Performance.* Plymouth, UK, Scarecrow press.

Williams, J. (2011). Inside the voice, Sing Up. http://www.singup.org/songbank/teaching-tools/teaching-resource-detail/view/50-inside-the-voice/

Education

Gardner, H. (1999). *Intelligence Reframed.* New York, Basic Books.

Hallam, S. (1998). *Instrumental Teaching: A Practical Guide to Better Teaching and Learning.* Oxford, Heinemann.

McPherson, G., Ed. (2006). *The Child as Musician,* Oxford University Press.

Rink, J., Ed. (2002). *Musical Performance: A Guide to Understanding.* Cambridge, Cambridge University Press.

Sloboda, J. A. (1985). *The Musical Mind.* Oxford, Clarendon Press.

Westney, W. (2003). *The Perfect Wrong Note.* Cambridge, Amadeus Press.

Special educational needs

Adamek, M. and Darrow, A.A. (2005). *Music in Special Education.* Silver Spring, MD: AMTA.

Baron-Cohen, S. (2008). *Autism and Asperger Syndrome.* New York, OUP.

Jaquiss, V. and Paterson, D. (2005). *Meeting SEN in the Curriculum: Music.* London, David Fulton Publishers.

Ockelford, A. (2008). *Music for Children and Young People with Complex Needs.* Oxford, Oxford University Press.

Oglethorpe, S. 2001. *Instrumental Music for Dyslexics.* London, Whurr Publishers.

Miles, T. and Westcombe, J. eds, (2001). *Music and Dyslexia: Opening New Doors.* London, Whurr Publishers.

Phonetics

International Phonetic Association (1999). *Handbook of the International Phonetic Association,* Cambridge, Cambridge University Press.

Roach, P. (2009). *English Phonetics and Phonology,* Cambridge, Cambridge University Press.

References

1. Lovetri, J. and E.M. Weekly, *Contemporary commercial music (CCM) survey: who's teaching what in nonclassical music.* Journal of Voice, 2003. 17(2): pp. 207–215.
2. Welch, G., D. Sergeant, and P.J. White, *Age, sex and vocal task as factors in singing 'in-tune' during the first years of schooling.* Bulletin of the Council for Research in Music Education, 1997. **133**: pp. 153–160.
3. Mithen, S., *The Singing Neanderthals.* 2006, Cambridge, Mass.: Harvard University Press.
4. Hallam, S., *The power of music: Its impact on the intellectual, social and personal development of children and young people.* International Journal of Music Education, 2010. 28(3): pp. 269–289.
5. Beck, R., et al., *Choral singing, performance perception and immune system changes in salivary immunoglobulin and cortisol.* Music Perception, 2000. 18(1): pp. 87–106.
6. Clift, S. and G. Hancox, *The significance of choral singing for sustaining psychological wellbeing: findings from a survey of choristers in England, Australia and Germany.* Music Performance Research, 2010. 3(1): pp. 79–96.
7. Kreuz, G., et al., *Effects of choir singing or listening on secretory immunoglobulin A, cortisol and emotional state.* Journal of Behavioural Medicine, 2004. 27(6): pp. 623–635.
8. Schellenberg, E.G., *Exposure to music: the truth about the consequences.* In: *The Child as Musician,* G. McPherson, Editor, 2006, OUP: Oxford.
9. Welch, G., et al., *The impact of Sing Up: an independent research-based evaluation - the story so far,* 2010, International Music Education Research Centre. Institute of Education, University of London: London.
10. Welch, G.F., et al., *Children's singing development, self-concept and sense of social inclusion.* In: *Researching the impact of the National Singing Programme 'Sing Up' in England: Main findings from the first three years (2007–2010)* 2010, International Music Education Research Centre, Institute of Education: London.
11. Cram, S., *The Young Athlete's Handbook.* 2001, Champaign, Il: Human Kinetics.
12. Welch, G. and D. Howard, *Gendered voice in the cathedral choir.* Psychology of Music, 2002. 30(1): pp. 102–120.
13. Ohala, J., *An ethological perspective on common cross-language utilisation of Fo of voice.* Phonetica, 1984. 41(1): pp. 1–16.
14. Sargeant, D. and G. Welch, *Perceived similarities and differences in the singing of trained children's choirs.* Choir Schools Today, 1997. 11: pp. 9–10.

15. Harrison, S., *Where have the boys gone? The perennial problem of gendered participation in music.* British Journal of Music Education, 2007. **24**(3): pp. 267–280.

16. Knight, S., *Exploring a cultural myth: what adult non-singers may reveal about the nature of singing.* In: *The Phenomenon of Singing ll*, B.A. Roberts and A. Rose, Editors, 1999, Memorial University Press: St Johns, NF.

17. Ternström, S. and J. Sundberg, *Acoustics of choir singing.* In: *Acoustics for Choir and Orchestra*, S. Ternström, Editor, 1986, Royal Swedish Academy of Music: Stockholm. pp. 12–22.

18. Howard, D., et al., *Are real-time displays of benefit in the singing studio? An exploratory study.* Journal of Voice, 2007. **21**(1): pp. 20–34.

19. Parncutt, R., *Prenatal development.* In: *The Child as Musician*, G. McPherson, Editor 2006, OUP: Oxford.

20. Trehub, S.E., L.A. Thorpe, and B.A. Morrongiello, *Organizational processes in infants' perception of auditory patterns.* Child Development, 1987. **58**: pp. 741–749.

21. Welch, G., D. Sergeant, and P.J. White, *The role of linguistic dominance in the aquisition of song.* Research Studies in Music Education, 1998. **10**: pp. 67–74.

22. Welch, G.F., *Singing and vocal development.* In: *The Child as Musician*, G. McPherson, Editor 2006, OUP: Oxford.

23. Gagné, R.M., L.J. Briggs, and W.W. Wager, *Principles of Instructional Design.* 4th Edition 1992, New York: Harcourt Brace Jovanovich.

24. Austin, J., J. Renwick, and G. McPherson, *Developing motivation.* In: *The Child as Musician*, G. McPherson, Editor, 2006, OUP: Oxford.

25. Gardner, H., *Intelligence Reframed.* 1999, New York: Basic Books.

26. McPherson, G. and A. Williamon, *Giftedness and talent.* In: *The Child as Musician*, G. McPherson, Editor, 2006, OUP: Oxford.

27. Morley, A.P., et al., *AVPR1A and SLC6A4 Polymorphisms in Choral Singers and Non-Musicians: A Gene Association Study.* PLoS ONE, 2012. 7(2): p. e31763. doi:10.1371/journal.pone.0031763.

28. Chaffin, R. and A. Lemieux, *General perspectives on achieving musical excellence,* in *Musical Excellence: Strategies and Techniques to Enhance Performance*, A. Williamon, Editor 2004, OUP: Oxford.

29. Walker, P., et al., *Preverbal infants' sensitivity to synaesthetic cross-modality correspondences.* Psychological Science, 2010. **21**(1): pp. 21–25.

30. Ludwig, V.U., I. Adachi, and T. Matsuzawa. *Visuoauditory mappings between high luminance and high pitch are shared by chimpanzees (Pan troglodytes) and humans.* in *Proceedings of the National Academy of Sciences.* 2011.

31. Welch, G.F., D. Sergeant, and P.J. White, *Age, sex and vocal tasks as factors in singing 'in-tune' during the first years of schooling.* Bulletin of the Council for Research in Music Education, 1997. **133**: pp. 153–160.

32. Welch, G.F., et al., *Sex, gender and singing development: Making a positive difference to boys' singing through a national programme in England.* In: *Perspectives on Males and Sing-*

ing, S. Harrison, G.F. Welch, and A. Adler, Editors, 2012, Springer: London. pp. 37–54.

33. Bennett, S., *A 3-year longitudinal study of school-aged children's fundamental frequencies.* Journal of Speech and Hearing Research, 1983. **26**: pp. 132–142.

34. Tarrant, M., et al., *Social identity in adolescence.* Journal of Adolescence, 2001. **24**: pp. 597–609.

35. Weiss, D.A., *The Pubertal Change of the Human Voice.* Folia Phoniatrica, 1950. **2**: pp. 128–159.

36. Gackle, L., *Understanding voice transformation in female adolescents*, in *Bodymind and Voice*, L. Thurman and G. Welch, Editors, 2000, The VoiceCare Network: Minnesota, USA. pp. 739–744.

37. Thurman, L. and G. Welch, eds. *Bodymind and Voice.* 2000, The VoiceCare Network.

38. Geithner, Woynarowska, and R. Malina, *The adolescent spurt and sexual maturation in girls active and not active in sport.* Annals of Human Biology, 1998. **25**(5): pp. 415–423.

39. Lã, F. *The effects of the menstrual cycle and the oral contraceptive pill on the female operatic singing voice.* in *PEVOC6.* 2005. London, UK: unpublished.

40. Harries, M.L., et al., *Changes in the male voice during puberty: speaking and singing voice parameters.* Logopedics Phoniatrics Vocology, 1996. **21**: pp. 95–100.

41. Cooksey, J.M., *Voice transformation in male adolescents.* In: *Bodymind and Voice*, L. Thurman and G. Welch, Editors. 2000, The VoiceCare Network: Minnesota, USA. pp. 718–738.

42. Cooksey, J.M., *Working with Adolescent Voices.* 1999, St Louis: Concordia.

43. Ashley, M., *The angel enigma: experienced boy singers' perceptual judgements of changing voices.* Music Education Research, 2011. **13**(3): pp. 343–354.

44. Williams, J., *Cathedral choirs in the United Kingdom: The professional boy chorister*, in *Perspectives on Males and Singing*, S. Harrison, G.F. Welch, and A. Adler, Editors, 2012, Springer: London.

45. Cooper, I., *Changing voices.* Music Educators Journal, 1962. **48**: pp. 148–151.

46. Swanson, F.J., *The Male Singing Voice Ages Eight to Eighteen.* 1977, Cedar Rapids, Iowa: Laurance Press.

47. Leck, H., *Creating artistry through choral excellence.* Methodology Chorals 2009: Hal Leonard.

48. Phillips, K., *Teaching Kids to Sing.* 1992, New York: Schirmer.

49. Iznaola, R., *On Practicing*, 1992, Aurora, CO: Iznaola Guitar Works.

50. Ginsborg, J., *Strategies for memorising music.* In: *Musical Excellence*, A. Williamon, Editor, 2004, OUP: Oxford.

51. Ginsborg, J., *Classical singers learning and memorising a new song: an observational study.* Psychology of Music, 2002. **30**(1): pp. 58–101.

52. Silverman, E.-M. and C.H. Zimmer, *Incidence of chronic hoarseness among school-age children.* Journal of Speech and Hearing Disorders, 1975. **40**: pp. 211–215.

53. Bonet, M. and P. Casan, *Evaluation of dysphonia in a children's choir.* Folia Phoniatrica, 1994. **46**: pp. 27–34.

54. Roy, N., et al., *Voice amplification versus vocal hygiene instruction for teachers with voice disorders.* Journal of Speech, Language and Hearing Research, 2002. **45**: pp. 625–638.

55. Titze, I.R., E. Hunter, and J.G. Svec, *Voicing and silence periods in daily and weekly vocalisations of teachers.* Journal of the Acoustical Society of America, 2007. **121**(1): pp. 469–479.

56. Hardy, L. and J. Fazey. *The Inverted-U Hypothesis: a catastrophe for sport psychology?* in *Annual Conference of the North American Society for the Psychology of Sport and Physical Activity.* 1987. Vancouver.

57. Garfield Davies, D. and A.F. Jahn, *Care of the Professional Voice.* 2nd edn, 2004, London: A & C Black.

58. Backus, B., T. Clark, and A. Williamon. *Noise exposure and hearing thresholds among orchestral musicians.* in *International Symposium on Performance Science.* 2007.

59. Williams, J., *The implications of intensive singing training on the vocal health and development of boy choristers in an English Cathedral Choir.* In: *Institute of Education,* 2010, University of London: London.

60. Hardy, L., G. Parfitt, and J. Pates, *Performance catastrophes in sport: a test of the hysteresis hypothesis.* Journal of Sports Sciences, 1994. **12**(4): pp. 327–334.

61. Baker, J., *Psychogenic voice disorders - heroes or hysterics? A brief overview with questions and discussion.* Logopedics Phoniatrics Vocology, 2002. **27**: pp. 84–91.

62. Brinson, P. and F. Dick, *Fit to Dance? The report of the national enquiry into dancers' health and injury,* 1996, Calouste Gulbenkian Foundation: London.

63. Chapman, J. *An English case study. The journey of a boy treble to Oxbridge choral scholar to adult professional soloist.* In: *PEVOC.* 1995. London.

64. Lloyd, P., *Let's all Listen,* 2008, London: Jessica Kingsley Publishers.

65. Mould, A., *The English Chorister: A History.* 2007, London: Hambledon Continuum.

66. Baragwaneth, N., *The Italian Traditions and Puccini.* 2011, Indiana: Indiana University Press.

67. The Musical Standard, 1871.

68. Cox, G., *Historical perspectives.* In: *The Child as Musician,* G. McPherson, Editor, 2006, OUP: Oxford.

69. Timesonline. http://entertainment.timesonline.co.uk/tol/arts_and_entertainment/article659914.ece. last accessed March 2009.

Index

abdomen, 84, 85, 87, 125, 140, 148
acoustic(s), 18, 80, 109, 119, 151, 152, 153, 154, 161, 170
adaptive anxiety, 166
alignment, 2, 81, 83, 117, 125, 134, 148, 191
allergies, 153, 160
alto, 70, 72, 73, 77, 92, 202
amplification, 119, 152, 170
amplitude (loudness), 28, 90, 119, 205
articulators, 120
Asperger's syndrome, 180, 185, 186, 187
asthma, 95, 124, 153, 158, 189
attention deficit hyperactivity disorder (ADHD), 36, 188
audiation, 17
audio recording, 74, 107, 148
autistic spectrum, 180, 187
automatisms, 37

baritone, 39, 54, 65, 69, 72, 77, 202
bass, 72, **74**, 202
belting, 95, **100–101**, 118, 202
Braille music, 191, 192
breath control, 37
breathiness, 59, 60, 76, 96, **97–98**, 118, 121, 124, 136, 173, 202
breathing, xxii, 3, 25, 26, 27, **30**, 44, 49, 60, 81–87, 90, 117, 124, 128, 134, 170, 176

abdominal, 60, 67, 117, 134
for anxiety management, 152, 153, 168, 169, 171
bronchitis, 95, 124

Cambiata, 70, 202
cartilage(s), 28, 65, 80, 88, 89, 104, 161, 202, 203, 208
arytenoid, 88, 92, 122, 161, 202, 207, 208, 210
cricoid, 88, 202, 203
thyroid, 59, 61, 69, 88, 92, 203, 208, 210
caustic ingestion, 161
cerebral palsy, **193**
cervical vertebrae, 29, 203
coloratura passages, 28, 50, 128
consonant(s), xxii, 106, 109, **112**, 115, 137
consonant problems, **113**, 118
constriction, xxii, 79, **94–95**, 103, 109, 111, 112, 118, 119, 135, 153, 189
contemporary commercial music (CCM), xvii, 94, 115, 118, 202, 203
Cooksey, John, 62, 63, 64, 70
Cooper, Irvin, 70
creak, **94**, 96, 98, 118
Curwen, John Spencer, 17, 18, 199
cystic fibrosis, **194**
cysts, 160

deconstriction, 60, 95, 96, 135, 136, 203, 206
diaphragm, xxi, 26, 27, 85, 87, 117, 128, 203
distractions, 36, 139, **182–183**, 188, 195
Down's syndrome, **193**
Dynamic(s), 3, 28, 50, 93,
dyscalculia, **184–185**
dyslexia, 180, **184–185**, 186
dysphonia, 11, 160, 161, 165, 203, 204
dyspraxia, 180, **184–185**

eczema, **189**
epiglottis, 25, 89, 90, 122, 155, 203
epilarynx, 122, 203, 209
epithelium, 45
evolution
  of singing, 1
  of the larynx, 13, 61, 76
exercise(s)
  technical, 141
  Head and Neck Exercise 1, 82
  Head and Neck Exercise 2, 82
  Head and Neck Exercise 3, 82
  Breathing Exercise 1, 83
  Breathing Exercise 2, 84
  Breathing Exercise 3, 84
  Belly Balancing Exercise, 86
  Larynx-loosening Wobble Exercise, 93
  De-constriction Exercise 1, 95
  De-constriction Exercise 2, 95
  De-constriction Detector 3: The Siren, 96
  Onset Exercise 1, 97
  Onset Exercise 2: Ski Jumps, 97
  Breathiness Exercise 1, 98
  Breathiness Exercise 2, 98
  Jaw Exercise 1, 105
  Jaw Exercise 2, 105
  Jaw Exercise 3, 105

Jaw and Tongue Root Exercise 1, 106
Tongue Root Exercise 2, 107
Resonance Exercise, 108
Soft Palate Exercise 1, 109
Soft Palate Exercise 2, 109
Vowel Exercise, 110
Consonant Exercise, 112
Register-bridging Exercise 1 or 4x4s, 115
Register-bridging Exercise: The Wicked Witch meets the Cowardly Lion, 116
Stress-buster Exercise, 169
Expiration (out-breath), **83–85**, 87, 169, 204

facial expression, **113**
falsetto, 19, 49, 63, 65, 67, 68, 70, 72, 74, 77, 90, **92–93**, 119, 136, 204, 207
fatigue-related conditions, 124, 190
formant(s), 61, 80, 109, 110, 119, 120, 121, 122, 175, 204, 208
frequency, 17, 20, 21, 49, 61, 63, 90, 93, 110, **119–122**, 128, 175, 204, 205, 207, 208, 210

Gardner, Howard, 40, 41
gastroesophageal reflux, 160
gender differences, **13–15**
glottis, 97, 119, 202, 204

Hackett, Maria, 198
harmonics, 104, 119, 120, 204, 209
hearing impairment, 17, 180, **190–191**
hyoid bone, 88, 106, 205, 208

inflammation, 118, 160, 165, 189
injury
  prevention of, 130, 132, 134, 141
inspiration, 84, 203, 205

instruments, 14, 123
  percussion, 46
intonation (or tuning), 10, 14, **16–19**,
      22, 28, 32, 34, 47–48, 112, 175,
      191, 205

jaw, 25, 26, 101, **104–105**, 106, 108,
      111, 113, 118, 120, 128, 137,
      175
  tension, 104, 105, 134

kinaesthetic awareness, 17, 19, 40,
      146, 185, 190, 205
kinaesthetic methods, 181, 182, 183,
      195
Kodály, Zoltán, 17, 18, 182, 198

laryngeal constriction, 79, 94, 95, 153,
      189, 205
larynx, xxi, xxii, 2, 9, 11, 13, 14, 16,
      25, 26, 28, 29, 34, 45, 49, 52,
      58, 59, 60, 61, 62, 65, 68, 70,
      71, 72, 73, 76, 78, 79, **88–90**,
      92, 93, 94, 99, 101, 102, 103,
      104, 106, 117, 119, 122, 135,
      136, 137, 141, 155, 161, 174,
      176, 203, 205, 206, 207, 208,
      209
Leck, Henry, 70
Legato, 182
limbic system, 9
long-term memory, 143, **182**, 184
loudness, 3, 37, 46, 49, 50, 52, 77, 79,
      86, 88, 90, 93, 117, 119, 129,
      164, 205, 208, 209
lungs, xxi, 25, 26, 27, 28, 34, 45, 58,
      85, 87, 88, 89, 135, 189, 194,
      205

memorisation, 5, 15, 30, **142–144**,
      146, 182, 184, 205
memory, 3, 37, 142, 143, 156
  episodic, 143

procedural, 143
  semantic, 143
modal voice, 92
Modified Staff Notation, 191
motivation, 15, 38, 39, **138–139**
motor memory, 37, 205
'Mozart effect', 4
mucosal layer, 90, 93, 206
mucosal wave, 90, 119, 206
muscle(s), xxi, xxii, 8, 9, 16, 17, 28,
      58, 65, 68, 69, 71, 72, 73, 79,
      83, 84, 85, 87, 88, 89, 91, 100,
      104, 109, 113, 117, 118, 128,
      131, 132, 133, 135, 136, 140,
      145, 152, 168, 176, 182, 189,
      205, 206, 207
  cricothyroid, 90
  deep neck flexor, 69, 203
  intercostal, 26
  laryngeal suspensory, 72, 79, 104,
      207
  lower abdominal, 83, 117
  pharyngeal constrictor, 69, 103
  strap, 104, 207
  thyroarytenoid, 90, 92
  vocalis, 92, 132, 208, 210
musical notation, 46, 198, 199
musical style, xvii, 3, 4, 60, 114, 116,
      118

nasality, **108–109**, 137
nodules, xxii, 160, 161

onset, 3, 10, 37, 60, 79, 94, **96–97**,
      98, 118, 136, 206
ornamentation, 10
overtones, 13, 19, 29, 46, 204, 206

pentatonic sequence, 16
Phillips, Kenneth, 70
pitch, xvi, 3, 13, 14, 16, 17, 18, 19,
      22, 23, 28, 29, 31, 32, 34, 37,
      46, 49, 50, 52, 59, 60, 61, 62,

pitch *continued*, 63, 64, 65, 67, 68, 69,
    70, 71, 72, 73, 74, 76, 77, 79,
    86, 90, 92, 93, 94, 99, 100, 111,
    112, 117, 119, 120, 128, 136,
    146, 150, 175, 186, 190, 191,
    199, 207
  accuracy, 13, 17, 18, 32, 47
pharyngeal constriction, 111
pharyngeal tone, 104
pharynx, **103–104**, 111, 118, 119,
    122, 135, 174, 175, 206, 209
phonemes, 22, 206
phonetic(s), xvii, 211
phrasing, 3, 10
Plato, 196
polyps, 160
posture, **30**, 34, 37, 44, 49, **81–87**,
    100, 104, 116, 117, 124, 134,
    139, 146
practice, 7, 8, 37, 42, 49, 51, 73, 74,
    123–129, **138–139**, 140, 141,
    144, 146, 183, 189, 207
psychomotor skill educational theory,
    35, 207
puberphonia, 64, 67, 207
puberty, xvi, xxiii, 13, 14, 28, **57–59**,
    60, 61, 70, 76, 94, 98, 194, 207
physical development, xxv, **25–28**,
    45, 194
  of body, 45
  of voice, 45, 59, 61

register, 54, 73, 90, 92, 99, 100, 115,
    116, 117, 209
  chest, 90, **92**, 209
  head, 90, **92**, 209
register change, 60, 97, **99–100**, 121
Reinke's space, 90, 92
repertoire, **4**, 47, **50**, 53, 57, 60,
    68–69, 72, 76, **78–79**, 100,
    115, 128, **141**, 145, 200, 207
repetition, 37, 38, 46, 80, 113, 143,
    182, 186

resonance, 29, 80, 98, 99, 108, 116,
    119, 120, 136, 137, 141
  projected, **107–108**, 118
resonators, xxii, 120
ribs, 26, 84, 85, 87

sensory store, 143
short-term memory, 143, **182**, 184
sight-reading, 16, 47, 124, 143, 145,
    175, 184
singing in tune, 16, 17, **32**, 47, 52
'Sing-Up' programme, 5, 47
soft palate, xxii, 25, 101, 102, 103,
    104, 108, 109, 111, 116, 118,
    120, 137, 174, 175, 207
soprano, 65, 66, 67, 70, 71, 72, **73**,
    74, 77, 119
sound waves, 104
speaking voice, 14, 32, 49, 61, 62, 63,
    64, 65, 66, 67, 68, 71, 73, 79,
    107, 124, 125, 145, 161, 165,
    207
speech, xxi, 1, 2, 15, 17, 18, 22, 23,
    26, 27, 28, 34, 49, 63, 89, 94,
    96, 99, 113, 115, 118, 137, 145,
    150, 161, 180, 190, 193, 205
  defects, 113
  therapy, 67, 68, 160
staccato, 182
stage fright, 166, 171
stamina, 3, 9, 11, 26, 49, 50, 52, 70,
    77, 78, 79, 128, 145, 194, 207
subglottic pressure, 90, 119
support, 86, 174, 208
swallowing, 25, 69, 94, **103**, 118, 128,
    135, 155, 157, 170, 203, 206,
    207
Swanson, Frederick, 70

tenor, 65, 66, 67, 68, **72**, 74, 77, 119,
    177
tessitura, 69
thick-fold singing, 100, 101, 115

thin-fold singing, 100, 136
throat, xxii, 2, 89, 90, 101, 106, 135,
    155, 156, 157, 158, 160, 174,
    175, 204, 206
tongue, xxii, 88, 96, 102, 103, 104,
    106–107, 109, 110, 111, 112,
    113, 115, 118, 120, 135, 137,
    138, 174, 175, 193, 208
    root, 11, 93, 96, 103, 106, 107, 109,
    112, 118, 135, 137, 175, 208
Tonic Sol-fa, 198, 199
treble, 54, 65, 66, 67, 70, 72
twang, 100, 101, 109, 122, 128, 208

upper partials, xxii, 90, 109, 186, 204,
    206, 208, 209

vibrato, 11, 93–94, 117, 208
visual gestures, 19
visual impairment, 180, 191–192
vocal
    fold(s), 26, 28, 45, 59, 62, 64, 72,
        79, 88, 90–92, 93, 94, 96, 97,
        99, 100, 101, 102, 117, 118,
        119, 121, 122, 136, 150, 155,
        156, 157, 158, 160, 202, 204,
        205, 206, 207, 208, 209, 210
    closure, 31, 72, 100
    collisions, 88, 90, 119, 150, 206
    nodules, xxiii
    pathology, 54
    tissue, 45, 90, 150
    gestures, 1, 8
    health, xxiii, 105, 149, 150, 155–
        172, 203, 209
    ligament, 45, 92, 93, 94, 204, 209

loading, 100, 101, 129, 150, 154,
    160, 164, 170, 209
range, 15, 66, 72, 77, 96, 99, 100,
    115, 191, 204, 209
structure, 28, 46
    of infant, 25–28, 34
    of young child, 28–30, 34
technique, 7, 8, 44, 57, 65, 73, 78,
    95, 116, 133, 138, 152
timbre, 3, 26, 30, 31, 60, 78, 90,
    110, 117, 209
tract, 2, 13, 14, 26, 29, 30, 50, 62,
    90, 101, 102, 103, 104, 108,
    109, 112, 118, 119–121, 174,
    175, 209, 210
voice
    change (in males), 45, 61, 62, 63,
        64, 65, 67, 69, 70, 71, 72, 74,
        76, 202
    disorders, 11, 149, 152, 160–161,
        165, 170, 171, 203
    loss, 8, 73, 149, 150, 160
vowel(s), xvii, xxii, 11, 22, 26, 62, 86,
    96, 97, 98, 102, 106, 109–111,
    112, 115, 118, 120, 121, 136,
    137, 138, 175, 206, 208
modification, 98, 121, 210
problems, 111
sounds, xvii, 101, 120, 211

warming up, xxi, 65, 130–134, 141,
    146
windpipe, 25, 88, 89, 103, 205

yawning, xxii, 103, 106, 118, 134,
    174, 175

CPSIA information can be obtained at www.ICGtesting.com
Printed in the USA
LVOW010914111012

3096LVUK00004B/3/P